a HISTORY *of* SCOTLAND

DAVID ROSS

WAVERLEY BOOKS

This edition published 2009 by Waverley Books
David Dale House, New Lanark, ML11 9DJ, Scotland

© Waverley Books 2009

Text by David Ross.
First published as *Pocket History of Scotland* by Geddes & Grosset.
Additional material in Chapter Eleven by Finlay McColl

ISBN 978 1 902407 97 5

Printed and bound in the UK

Contents

a HISTORY *of* SCOTLAND

Introduction

Short histories, particularly when dealing with earlier centuries, often seem to consist of little more than accounts of kings, queens and battles. Although it was once the normal thing for kings – and sometimes queens – to direct events, in the historical record they often unduly overshadow their own times, and receive credit or discredit for things for which they were not responsible. In writing this short history, an effort has been made to keep the kings and queens in perspective, and to hold the focus as much as possible on the people. Some 70 generations have inhabited Scotland within historical time. It is their work, their beliefs and their experience which form the basis of modern Scotland. With a healthy admixture from new arrivals through the centuries, their genes are still present and contribute, together with the long and varied national tradition, to define the Scottish people. In a real sense, their story is ours, and our story is theirs.

CHAPTER ONE

From Tundra Hunters to Celtic Tribes – Prehistoric Scotland

Experts on the prehistory of Scotland have put the population of the country around 7000 BC as low as a few hundred, even a few dozen. A thousand or so years before that, the landscape was probably not habitable at all – a wilderness of roaring water, vast lakes, marshland, and tundra-type plants on the higher ground. Insects would be the most obvious forms of life. Melted ice-caps and glaciers left a stripped and scraped surface, with great piles of raw gravel and soil residue as if the whole place had been an open-cast mine. Boulders and smaller stones littered the land surface in their millions. Gradually, time, weather and vegetation softened this landscape somewhat, proper trees like birch and hazel began to grow, birds, fish and animals began to colonise, and in pursuit of these arrived the great predator species, the human hunters.

The First Inhabitants

Before the last ice age, and during its occasional warmer spells, the area may have been inhabited, but the complete icing up meant that a new start was necessary. Continuous human and other life in Scotland is much more recent than in Europe and even than in other parts of the British Isles. The first inhabitants are likely to have come up from, or through, England – separated from Europe then by a great river rather than the open sea – or from Ireland, or perhaps across what had not yet become the North Sea: a complex basin of water channels, lagoons, pools, marshes, islands and sand dunes. The evidence of stone blades from the Mesolithic period does not give a clear guide as to the points of departure, and it may be that groups of people converged on Scotland from all three directions. If they came from the south, they had to learn new things about living. They had moved across the edge of a different zone of existence, known as the circumpolar region – an area of habitation south of the Arctic Circle, spanning the narrow curve of the earth's shoulder between latitudes 55 and 65, and taking in Labrador, Scandinavia and Siberia. Climate ruled life here. Humans had to take account of long winters, and may at first have been only summer visitors, migrating south when the autumn equinox heralded the annual freeze.

Their scanty equipment was portable; their buildings were lightweight and temporary wigwams. Eventually some family groups began to stay in favourite locations. Still nomadic, they roamed over districts a few square miles across. Their camp sites were transient and flimsy but traces of them have been found in many parts of the country. These people were members of the same species as ourselves, with the endowments of language, laughter and imagination. Physically shorter and stockier than the modern average, with more powerful jaws, they were already lords of creation. Their technology is classified as Mesolithic, the middle period of the Stone Age, which lasted from around 7000–4000 BC. Their technical skills – carving, sewing, tracking, trapping, throwing, catching – would in most respects eclipse those of almost all modern peoples, though many of these abilities and techniques survived, some virtually unchanged, into the nineteenth century.

By 5000 BC, human occupancy, though very sparse, covered the whole mainland and the islands. One of the oldest known settlements was on Rum, at Kinloch, and other island sites have been identified on Oronsay and Jura as well as in Orkney. While most sites have been found in coastal locations, others have been discovered as far inland as Banchory in Aberdeenshire and Dryburgh in the Tweed valley. Evidence of stone blade-chipping and fire-marked earth are the main markers, along with occasional midden heaps.

The generations that elapsed between 5000 BC and the start of the Common (or Christian) era, allowing 30 years for each, number over 160. Probably 20 years is a better estimate, making the number of generations more like 250. A brief moment in geological time, a slightly longer one in human evolution – a long, slow era of human cultural and technical continuity. During those many generations, profound changes in human society occurred, including the gradual start of acceleration of the human mastery of technology. At the end of this period, a dweller in Scotland would inhabit a landscape, a society and a world very different from those of an ancestor who lived at the beginning. Yet most if not all of these generations would scarcely have been aware of change in their lifetimes.

The inhabitants of prehistoric Scotland were not pace-setters. Placed as they were, at the outer edge of the western world, it was perhaps scarcely to be expected that it should be otherwise. It was hard making a reasonable life from stony ground under cold grey skies, and time for reflection and innovation was at a premium. Most new things came to them, rather than originating among them. These included the kind of improvements in tool-making and other activities that saw the Mesolithic way of life slowly give way to that of the Neolithic, the 'New Stone Age'. The whole country was densely forested with elm, oak and pine. The woodland was a huge resource but also an obstacle. Neolithic inhabitants vigorously began the long attack on Scotland's forest cover, clearing space for cultivation and for grazing, driving back the wolves and bears.

Neolithic Settlements, Tombs and Stone Circles

The Neolithic period saw the beginnings of farming. Communities ceased to be wholly dependent on hunting-gathering, which involved a nomadic circuit round a range of sites, and became settled in one area, where they planted crops and kept animals. A settled society acquired a new set of needs and imperatives. Since the whole family group no longer had to travel, dwellings could be permanent and solid. Possessions could increase and be more substantial. New tools were needed. New utensils, pots and jars, were made and put to use. Most of the knowledge required for this was probably brought in by new settlers. But there were other types of contact too. Far back in prehistory, people were already travelling large distances to find resources such as special kinds of very hard, or very soft, stone. The process of cultural transmission, in which new techniques, new beliefs, new speech habits, spread year by year, through adjacent communities, is a very ancient one.

Perhaps pigs and dogs were already being tamed, but the knowledge of sheep, cattle and goat breeding came from Europe, as did that of cereal cultivation, beginning with emmer wheat and barley. In Scotland, with a tiny population and rich food resources in forest, river, loch and sea, the development of farming might have been very slow, except that it offered a crucial improvement in the way of life – a harvest that yielded a winter food supply. A farming-hunting community had a much better chance of survival than a hunting-gathering one.

The Neolithic communities were the first to engage in substantial building work, and the largest structures were for the burial of the dead and for the rites associated with burial. Burial sites of various kinds are found all over the country and, paradoxically, are usually much easier to identify than the house-sites of the villagers who built them. The burial rituals of the Mesolithic inhabitants are unknown; their Neolithic descendants and successors clearly shared the same obsession with death – and, presumably, an after-life – as other communities of the same epoch, stretching geographically back through Europe to Egypt and the Near East. In their various forms – long barrows, round barrows, long cairns, chambered cairns – the tombs of our Neolithic ancestors reveal a sense of possession and permanence far different to the light and elusive imprint of the first inhabitants.

The variation in tomb construction, as with the variations in pottery and tool finds, suggests that the Neolithic inhabitants were not a homogeneous group with a single set of cultural beliefs, indicating again the diversity of original sources. A number of different languages may have been spoken. In the 2,000 years or so of the Neolithic period, between c. 4000–2000 BC, there was ample time for a whole succession of cultural changes to come and go (later, between AD 800 and 1300, the inhabitants of Fife would speak three different languages, Pictish, Gaelic and Scots). In the early Neolithic, the eastern regions built earthen barrows, sometimes round-shaped, sometimes extended in length, as well as stone cairns. On the western side, stone cairns often were heaped over an inner burial chamber. This practice, first found in the Western Isles, reached a peak with the building of the Maes Howe megalithic tomb in Orkney.

Most of the buildings were of wood, and evidence for them is scanty in the extreme, not least because settlements tended to be on the best available land, which has been occupied, worked over and built on for thousands of years. The clearest evidence – though certainly not typical in constructional style and perhaps not in other ways – comes from Orkney, where the Neolithic settlement of Skara Brae, with its little stone houses and stone furnishings, offers a window into the far-off past. An older two-house complex has also been excavated at Knap of Howar, on Papa Westray. It too is formed from stone slabs. The occupants used pottery jars, both coarse and decorated, but any evidence of wood, fur, cloth or bone materials has long disintegrated. The middens reveal a diet of sheep and cattle meat, fish and shell-fish. A few barley grains indicate limited cereal cultivation.

The dead have to be disposed of, one way or another, and although the chambered tombs and megalithic structures must have been an immense effort for small communities to build, they have an apparent purpose. The other great relics of the Neolithic period – the hundreds of stone circles and henge monuments which were set up throughout the country – have no such clear function, though some, as at Clava near Inverness, surround a chambered cairn.

The typical henge is a circular platform surrounded by a ditch and outer bank. Some (Class I) have a single entrance; others (Class II) have another access at the opposite side. Some have or had complete stone circles, like the Ring of Brogar in Orkney; others had different arrangements of standing or recumbent stones; or, as at Balfarg in Fife, had timber uprights, presumably supporting a structure within the circle. Exploration of the Stenness circle site in Orkney has revealed remnants of charcoal, burnt bone and pottery, and the flat stone platform at its centre has been considered as a sacrificial altar.

The labour required for these henges was far greater than that needed to build a cairn. It has been suggested that they were set up by groups of communities working together. This in turn implies a central direction of some sort, and has led to speculation on social hierarchies, priest-kings and precursors of the druids. But all this is pure conjecture based on the structural remains. It has long been clear, though, that astronomical knowledge was used in the siting of stone circles, and that the position of the sun was significant – most famously in the way it shines through the entrance passage of the Maes Howe tomb at the winter solstice. The builders and users of these structures had the time, resources and imagination to develop forms of ritual which were at least partly based on precise observation of the cosmos.

Bronze Age Communities

From around 2000 BC, evidence of a new decorated pottery style can be found in the south and east of the country. Its makers were formerly identified as a people of newcomers, the 'Beaker Folk', though notions of a widespread invasion have now been generally discounted in favour of cultural transmission. Other changes in social behaviour were occurring around the same time, including the abandonment of the monumental communal tombs in favour of individual burial in stone tombs, known as cists. An unknown but fundamental shift of ideology must have accompanied this practice, just as modern secularism has made cremation increasingly popular again.

Elsewhere in the world, the age of metal use had arrived, and by around 2000 BC, the technique of bronze-working had reached as far as Scotland. Bronze was the first hard metal to be worked. It is an alloy of copper and tin; Scotland had numerous deposits of the former but none of the latter. The tin mines of Cornwall were already operating, and the prehistoric inhabitants of Scotland joined the queue of customers. How the trade was arranged and financed is not known, but Scotland had gold and silver deposits, and perhaps also tusks, ambergris (a strongly scented substance from the intestines of sperm whales that would be collected from the sea or shore and used in making perfumes), pelts and feathers to offer.

More intensive exploitation of resources included use of the land itself. The advantages of using manure were identified and put into action, increasing productivity in the small fields and promoting the stability of the settlement. Social hierarchies became more developed. However egalitarian, or communistic, earlier society had been, the trend now was towards an aristocratic chieftain-led society. This is clearly seen in central Europe and in the contemporary Wessex culture of south-west England.

Bronze had given humans the sharpest edge yet found, and they were not slow to employ it in weaponry. As communities became larger and wealthier, and less preoccupied by the sheer need to provide themselves with a subsistence living, they became more aware of one another. Rivalry, envy and fear played a greater part in their relationships. The mobility and speed of the horse, the improvement of weapons, the evolution of a warrior caste which did not have to trouble itself with the basics of farming – all encouraged the development of a society that was preoccupied by warfare. Although in fact the amount of actual warfare was probably very small, its cultural importance was relatively much greater. Its effect would be to bring isolated communities into larger groupings, either by conquest or by combining for defence.

In these Bronze Age communities, we can perceive the origins of the 'Celtic' society which the invading Romans would encounter in Scotland, though that meeting was still more than 1,500 years away.

The communities themselves, even if settled in a particular district, were still mobile in one vital way, as indeed they would remain for many centuries to come. Farming was chiefly pastoral, and the movement of stock between the deep valleys and the upper slopes and high plateaux was a major consideration. Until around 1600 BC, the uplands were inhabited to about 400 metres (1,200 feet) or higher in sheltered places. Many graves are found at this level. After this time, there was a progressive deterioration of the climate. This was particularly marked in Ireland, an important source of trade in earlier times, which now suffered a serious reduction in population with much of the land reverting to forest again. A similar pattern in Scotland is detectable from a number of sources. Colder, wetter and windier weather drove the population, both human and animal, downhill. Conditions favoured the growth of peat over wide areas. Forest trees were prematurely felled by choking moss or by gales. Use of the uplands became much more seasonal, with a transfer to the high ground only for the summer months. Archaeological remains suggest a degree of impoverishment, with little to be found between around 1400 BC and the advent of the use of iron. Burial sites are hard to trace and their contents are scanty.

The Celts

The development of Celtic culture in Scotland was formerly identified with the arrival in the country of 'Celtic' colonists, who brought with them not only a language and customs which had developed in continental Europe, but also the secret of iron-working. Their possession of this latest step in human technology enabled them to achieve dominance over the already established inhabitants. Since the abandonment of this invasion theory, the consequent rather neat explanation has had to be reconsidered and a somewhat more complex picture emerges.

From 1200 BC or earlier, there was a people, or peoples, who lived in south central Europe and who were later identified both by Greeks and Romans as 'Celts'. This was a very broad definition, comparable with that of 'Scythians' for the peoples who lived to the north of the

Celts, in a band of Europe stretching from Scandinavia far into Russia. There are few references to the Celts before around 400 BC. The language, or languages, that they spoke belonged to the Indo-European family, as did Greek, Latin and the later Germanic tongues. There were a number of similarities between it and the Italic group which included Latin, though whether these were caused by two sets of language speakers living in proximity with each other, rather than any kind of joint descent from a single ancestral Indo-European language, is a matter for speculation. What is clear is that by around 1000 BC early forms of the Celtic speech had evolved, and by 600 BC were being spoken in the Iberian peninsula, in Ireland and in North Italy.

Historians of the ancient world have identified a period of dramatic change around the year 1200 BC. In a relatively short space of time the east Mediterranean civilisation, which included the wealthy and advanced kingdoms of Minoan Crete, Mycenae, and of the Hittites in Asia Minor, entered a state of collapse. Channels of trade and international contacts were disrupted, resulting in a shift northwards of the dynamic centre of power and trade to central Europe. The 'Urnfield' culture of this area, so-called because of the large-scale burial sites that have been found with the burnt remains of the cremated bodies placed in urns, is known to have been a warrior society, with the strong emphasis on personal display that is almost invariably found with such a system: 'The great bronze cauldrons, bronze and gold cups decorated in repoussé style and the elaborate weapon sets of the Urnfield period are the outward and visible signs of these otherwise hidden social systems' (Barry Cunliffe, *The Celts*, 25).

As the Urnfield civilisation spread, so its demand for imported raw materials grew greater and its own influence radiated out across a vast area of northern and north-western Europe. Such influence was generated not only by its commercial demands but also by its innovations in art and social life. In all fields, including religion, its prestige would have been great, and there would be much respectful and enquiring interest from far afield in the way of life exemplified by the increasingly flamboyant courts of the magnates. Much of the trade was organised on a sort of 'pass-it-on' basis, from community to community, until the goods reached their destination. Knowledge was handed on in much the same fashion. The process of language expansion went along the same lines, perhaps stimulated by enthusiasm to acquire the new speech. In the words of Professor Barry Cunliffe: '... if the socio-religious package of Urnfield practice, with its attendant infrastructure of language, was thought to be desirable as a mode of élite expression, then it would have been quickly assimilated into the culture of the Atlantic communities' (*The Celts*, 28). Scotland formed part of this Atlantic zone.

In the later Bronze Age, during the eighth and seventh centuries BC, a dynamic form of the Urnfield culture arose in the Austrian mountains, supported by the wealth generated from the salt deposits of Hallstatt. Salt was already a precious mineral resource, vital in food preserving and preparation. In addition to bronze, iron began to be worked here, perhaps from as early as the eighth century, the techniques imported from further east. A Hallstatt sword was a powerful totem as well as a dangerous weapon and, from the later Hallstatt period, swords were exported as far away as Ireland. Local smiths copied the designs and the Hallstatt pattern was reproduced in many places. The cemetery site at Hallstatt, when excavated, revealed remarkable burials of high-status goods, including a wheeled cart and much horse gear.

Metalworking had always been a highly specialised craft, practised by a small number of workers and no doubt closely supervised by the rulers. The advent of iron enhanced this specialism. The new metal was so much more effective, adaptable and durable than bronze that it might have been seen as having magic qualities even without the deliberate creation of a cult around the activities of the blacksmith (who would become an important and honourable figure in the Celtic community).

By the later centuries BC, with the expansion of Greek colonies and the rise of Republican Rome, the centre of continental Celtic culture had moved further west. It is typified by the site of La Tène, on Lake Neuchatel in Switzerland, close to the north-south trading route that stretched between the Greek city of Massilia (Marseille) on the Mediterranean Sea, and the coasts of north-west Europe. The La Tène culture arose around the fifth century BC and lasted until the first century and the Roman invasions of Gaul. La Tène was to have an influence on 'insular Celtic' art in Britain and Ireland long after it had been subsumed into the Gallo-Roman civilisation.

The inhabitants of Scotland were on the periphery of this thousand-year flourishing of Celtic language and Celtic art within the heart of Europe. Not only that, after about 600 BC, there is very little evidence of the kind of relations that had existed earlier. This has been linked to the continued climatic deterioration, again particularly serious in Ireland, and these centuries of relative isolation have been attributed to the preservation there of a more archaic form of Celtic language than that of continental Europe and of Britain.

What language or languages were spoken by the inhabitants of Scotland before they adopted a Celtic form, we do not know, any more than we can be certain of the process by which the Celtic form spread through the population. We can surmise that this happened first with the upper levels of society and was gradually picked up, generation by generation, by the rest. It is notable, though, that in the first century the Romans found that essentially the same language was spoken throughout the whole of Britain south of the Forth-Clyde line in Scotland. This language has been labelled Brittonic or Brythonic. It stems from the 'Common Celtic' that also evolved into the Gaulish language. Both share the linguistic changes that Irish Gaelic never adopted, notably the change of the k- or qu- sound into p- . Thus 'four' in Welsh became *pedwar*, whilst in Gaelic it was *ceithir*, closer to the Latin form *quattuor;* 'head' in Welsh became *pen,* whilst in Gaelic it was *ceann*; hence the often-found references to the languages as being p-Celtic and q-Celtic respectively.

It is important to bear in mind that Brittonic came to be spoken by the same people whose ancestors had lived in Scotland for many generations previously. Any admixture of colonists from Europe was likely to be so small as to be of imperceptible influence. (An exception to this may be in the north, both the mainland and the northern isles. The residual fragments of the Pictish language spoken there suggest a closer relationship to continental Gaulish than to insular Brittonic, leading some scholars to hint at a continental point of departure to a northern location for the Picts, or some of them.) Incomers from Ireland – unless, as is possible, there were groups in Ireland who spoke a p-Celtic language – are also unlikely. As most scholars are nowadays concerned to stress, it is only in the area of language that the word 'Celtic' has any real objective meaning.

Among the concepts imported from the Hallstatt culture was that of fortification. Prior to the seventh century, it is likely that the inhabitants were more concerned to protect their settlements from the attacks of wild animals than from the attacks of other communities. A simple palisade of stakes is likely to have been the protection for most homes. In central Europe, however, where riches and rivalries were greater, protection from one another became more important. Hill-forts, surrounded by massive ramparts, were established, often with whole 'towns' inside for the population to reside, or seek protection, in. Hill-forts had already been established in Scotland, perhaps as early as 1000 BC, but in the middle of the millennium, their numbers increased rapidly. The builders of these forts were principally shepherds, though they also cultivated wheat, barley and flax in small fields where shelter allowed. Evidence of metalworking has also been found at some fort sites, such as Craig Phadrig at Inverness and Dunadd in Argyll; at these the patronage and protection of a local chief or king allowed the bronze- and tin-smiths to practise their craft in security. Many forts were used only on particular occasions, such as special assemblies for trade or ritual purposes, apart from serving as refuges. Over the centuries they were often rebuilt, extended or reduced.

The huts within the forts, ranging in number from one or two to 150 or more, were round houses. A thick wall of stones and turf, with a single entrance, provided a base for a pitched roof of thatch, with a central smoke-hole for the fire. The building of hill-forts effectively came to an end with the Roman occupation.

Until recently, historians also linked the introduction of iron-working into Scotland with the arrival of a 'Celtic' people, whose iron weapons and tools were an important factor in their achieving domination over the inhabitants who were still practising a Bronze Age technology. The notion of the sudden importation of iron-working has been abandoned in favour of that of a much more gradual process, identical to that which also transmitted changes of language and culture. Even in later Iron Age sites, it is normal to find implements of bone and stone, clearly still in daily use, as well as of iron.

CHAPTER TWO

From Roman Invasion to National Unity, AD 78–1034

The inhabitants of Scotland in the year AD 78 were partly the descendants of those who had lived through the Stone and Bronze Ages, and into the Iron Age, and partly the descendants of more recent arrivals. They had become much more numerous, up to a quarter of a million or more. The isolated families or village communities of earlier times had coalesced into larger tribal groups. They were warlike people, though farming, fishing and hunting and the needs of community life must have taken up most of their time. Probably used to fighting with one another in boundary disputes, they had never faced invasion until, in AD 79, the Roman army appeared.

Rome had already conquered most of England and Wales and established a province of the Roman empire, called Britannia after the inhabitants' own name for it. The Roman aim was to extend their empire throughout the British mainland, but the combined resistance of the northern tribes and the landscape thwarted them. Under the governor, Agricola, they made a determined effort in AD 84, forcing the tribes into a pitched battle at a site known as Mons Graupius – now considered to be Bennachie in Aberdeenshire. The Romans won the battle but not the war. The defeated tribesmen fled, but there was no submission, and the Romans, after reaching the Moray Firth coast, withdrew.

Thirty-eight years later, the emperor, Hadrian, ordered a wall to be built across the northern end of the Roman province. The most massive frontier structure in the empire, much of it can still be seen. An area of Roman influence stretched to the north of it, and 20 years afterwards, in AD 143, a new frontier wall was built between the firths of Forth and Clyde, named by historians Antonine's Wall after the reigning emperor, Antoninus Pius. Between the walls was a zone under military control. But Antonine's Wall could not be sustained against the hostility of the tribes to the north. By AD 180, the frontier had moved back to Hadrian's Wall. Although Roman imperial armies would again invade, in 208 and 305, reaching almost as far as Agricola had in 78, the region north of the Antonine Wall remained intractable. It was never subdued by the Romans, something that would long be remembered with satisfaction, though some later scholars have regretted the consequent long extension of 'Iron Age' primitivism.

Tribal Groups

Around the time that the Antonine Wall was first stormed, far away in Alexandria, a Greek scientist, Ptolemy, was assembling current knowledge on world geography. His research on northern Britain gives numerous names of locations and tribes, with 17 of the latter occupying the territory of Scotland. The Romans called the area north of the Antonine wall Caledonia, after the largest tribe (or tribal group), the *Caledonii*, or Caledonians. A hundred years later a new name would appear in Roman writing, the *Picti*, or Picts.

To a great degree Picts and Caledonians must have been the same people, though some writers have suggested that the change of name indicates a political change in these regions, with dominance shifting from a people based south of the Mounth to one from north of it.

As the western empire of Rome gradually weakened and crumbled, the Picts, allied with tribes from Ireland, launched more and more wide-ranging attacks into the Roman province of Britannia, reaching as far as the capital city of Londinium. In the year 410, Roman rule ended and the provincials were left to defend themselves not only against the Picts but against Germanic tribes from across the North Sea. The Romano-British people put up a fierce resistance.

Scotland's population in the fifth century was made up of several different peoples. North of a line from Stirling to Dumbarton, and in the islands, were the Picts, who may have been themselves more than one people, speaking more than one language. South of the line, on the east, was a Brittonic-speaking tribe, the Votadinnii or Gododdin, who had always been the most Roman-friendly of the tribes. West and south-west were three tribes, the Selgovae, Novantae and Damnonii. In the course of the fifth and sixth centuries, this picture would change. Most stable was Pictland, though in its south-west corner, Lorn and the adjacent islands, a colony of Gaelic-speaking Scots from Ireland was established around AD 500, called Dàl Riada after their own tribal name. The south-western tribes amalgamated themselves into the strong Brittonic-speaking kingdom of Strathclyde, with its capital on Dumbarton Rock. The Votadinii were carrying on and gradually losing a war with invading Angles, a Germanic-speaking people who had established a fortress at Bamburgh, just south of the Tweed estuary.

By the end of the sixth century, the south-east was under Anglian control, with a strong-point established at Dunbar. Dàl Riada had expanded, and a strong Gaelic influence was being felt in the southern parts of Pictland, especially Strathearn and Atholl. Britons, Scots, Picts and Angles all held grimly to their territory, with much frontier fighting. As Germanic kingdoms to the south grew larger, they began to exert their influence to the north. The Anglian foothold at Bamburgh had swelled into the powerful kingdom of Northumbria, which conquered the Scots and southern Pictland in the mid-seventh century. Its imperial aims were finally crushed at Dunnichen in Angus, in 685, by a Pictish army under King Nechton, in a battle as decisive as Bannockburn in 1314. But from then on, no Scottish kingdom could overlook the threat from the more populous and powerful states south of the Cheviots.

A fifth element joined the struggle in the late eighth century, when the Norsemen began to raid the coasts. Soon they were establishing settlements. By the later ninth century, they had colonised and were ruling in

Shetland, Orkney and Caithness. Pictish culture was virtually obliterated in the northern isles and many people fled to the mainland.

The pressures on all kingdoms were enormous. Even though numbers of inhabitants were still relatively small, the amount of good cultivable land was not great. At this time, the climate was passing through a long mild spell, which may have encouraged settlement on higher ground, but this did not last into the eleventh century. The basis of dispute in Scotland would always come back to land-tenure. But other causes of dissension were present.

Pagans and Christians

The Norsemen were pagans and practitioners of some particularly bloody rites. The Angles, the Strathclyde Britons and the Dàl Riada Scots were Christians. By the time of the Viking invasions the Picts too were largely Christian. Among them, and probably in other kingdoms, many remnants of a pagan, druidic nature-religion still remained. Different religions, languages, social customs added to the climate of hostility. The Scots were as much preoccupied by events in Ireland as by those in their new home; frequent expeditions were necessary to assert control there.

Picts, Scots and Britons, despite their differences, shared much in the way of culture and social organisation. The foundations of their societies all went back to the 'Celtic' aristocratic pattern. At the topmost social level, royal families formed in effect a super-caste, intermarrying with one another and maintaining, through extended families, a strong control on the societies they ruled. The king's role was a dual one, of practical war-leader and of mystic intermediary between the people and the gods or powers of the natural world and the cosmos. When the nature-based religious cult maintained by the druids was replaced by Christianity, this latter role of the king was diminished but did not stop. Just as the senior druids would come from his close kindred, so the bishop of the tribe or kingdom would be a family member. No dividing line was drawn between the secular and the spiritual. Perhaps the prime example of this was Columcille, abbot of Iona from 563 to his death in 597, and a leading power-broker among the Gaelic kingdoms and tribal groups as well as a dedicated and saintly churchman, known to posterity as St Columba.

Christianity spread from small Romano-British communities south of Hadrian's Wall into the lands to the north. The first Christian site was probably at Whithorn, 'Candida Casa', established in the fourth century and associated with the name of St Ninian (died c. 431). It was a mission station which sent out intrepid messengers into the wild lands to the north. In 432, Patrick, a Briton, established his mission to Ireland and a few years later, Ireland was sending missionaries back again. The 'Celtic' church, never a centralised body, established a network of abbeys in Ireland, Wales, Strathclyde, Dàl Riada and Pictland, among which the monks moved freely. Among these abbeys, Iona, perhaps a sacred place from prehistory, had a special sanctity as the burial-place of kings, both Scottish and Pictish. The era was an age of saints, whose personal courage, austerity and devotion won them converts, and whose names are still preserved in many place-names, as with St Luoc in Kilmaluag, St Maelrubha in Loch Maree, St Mungo in Strathbungo.

The church had its own troubles and tensions. Having preserved the Christian tradition through the 'Dark Ages' of the fifth and sixth centuries, some of its practices had diverged from those of Rome. In the seventh century, as the Roman church sought to extend its control, there was controversy between the Celtic church and the new Roman-founded bishopric of Canterbury in England. In 663, at a synod convened at Whitby in Yorkshire, the issues were debated; the practice of the church in Northumbria would depend on the result. The Celtic monks were defeated, but a century or more would elapse before the Roman practice was fully accepted among them. Before that, in 710, there was a time of crisis when the Pictish king, Nechton, expelled all the Iona-trained clergy from his kingdom, and asked for help from the Northumbrian church. This has been put down to fears of Scottish priests exercising undue political influence in the Pictish kingdom.

The MacAlpin Dynasty

After Nechton's time, it was not unusual for Scots and the southern Picts to be ruled by the same king (almost nothing is known of life and politics north of the Great Glen at that time). But the identities of the kingdoms were kept separate until 843, when Kenneth MacAlpin, who had made himself King of Scots in 839, also assumed the kingship of the Picts. From then on, the Gaelic-speaking Scots held the initiative. The Pictish language began to go out of use. This was also the time of the most serious Viking invasions, when Dàl Riada was being harried from the sea and the Pictish provinces invaded by land armies. Trouble with the Vikings would go on for almost another 400 years, though there would be occasional alliances and phases of co-operation as well.

A difficulty in interpreting the history of Scotland during this period is that the sources, monastic records rewritten in the eleventh century or later, are so sparse in their information and offer little more than a list of kings, abbots and battles, with the occasional plague or exceptional spell of weather. It would be easy to infer a state of almost permanent warfare. But this is certainly not the full story. Fighting was probably on a relatively small scale – an army of 2,000 would have been a substantial one – and localised, and confined largely to summer. The Vikings themselves were known as 'summer-raiders'. An agriculture-based society had to attend to spring planting and sowing, and to the harvest, in order to survive from one year to the next. There is also evidence, in the carved stone-work of Pictland in the seventh to ninth centuries, of a strong artistic tradition supported by royal or lordly patronage. Some of the finest sculpture comes from a district wide open to attack from the sea, the Tarbat peninsula of Easter Ross. There must have been long peaceful periods; some areas may never have experienced warfare at all, whilst others had more than their share. Iona was ravaged by Norse attacks at least three times between 795 and 806, and raids continued until in 818 the monks left the island in despair.

Kenneth MacAlpin and his successors had already established their centre of power in the east. Scone, Forteviot and Abernethy were among the royal centres. The establishment of a Norse kingdom of the Hebrides confirmed this shift, and the ecclesiastical centre moved from Iona first to Dunkeld, then, briefly, Abernethy; and then to the Celtic monastery site of Cinnrighmonaidh in East Fife, around which a bold legend had arisen, in the course of the tenth century, that the bones of the apostle St Andrew had been landed here, in the care of the Greek monk, Regulus. A church of St Regulus was built, and then a cathedral dedicated to St Andrew, from which the surrounding township took its later name of St Andrews. It seems likely that there was substantial movement of Scots into Pictland, both across the southern fringe of the Highlands into Strathearn and Pictland; and up through the Great Glen into Moray. This latter movement, from the tribal region of Lorn, may have set up a Gaelic-Pictish kingdom in Moray which did not acknowledge the superiority of the MacAlpin kings.

To be king was a risky trade: three MacAlpin kings died fighting the Vikings, one was killed fighting the Strathclyde Britons, and others fell to internal strife.

Despite the loss of Caithness, Sutherland, the islands, and parts of Argyll to the Norsemen, the Scottish-Pictish kingdom survived. The Strathclyde Britons did not. In 871, a siege mounted from the Viking base at Dublin sacked the royal centre at Dumbarton and yielded a great amount of booty and many slaves. Strathclyde never recovered; although it remained an independent kingdom, it fell increasingly under the influence of the Scots. Its king, Artgal, was killed in 872 at the instigation of the Scottish king, Constantine. His son and grandson ruled after him; the next king was Owen, who despite his Cumbric name was a scion of the MacAlpins. Following this Scottish take-over, many of the Cumbric-speaking nobility and their followers moved to join their co-linguists in Wales. From then until 1034, Strathclyde was a client state of the northern power named Scotia or Alba.

The MacAlpins were a determined and acquisitive dynasty – undoubtedly the most successful to occupy the throne of Scotland. Not that this meant a peaceful line of succession – primogeniture (the succession of the first-born male) was not practised, and the eligible members of the royal family frequently fought each other for the throne. At times, especially in the middle of the tenth century, it looked as if the unifying tendency might fall apart. But when kings were secure, events to the south engaged their attention.

The development of the Anglo-Saxon kingdoms, disrupted by the establishment of the Danish kingdom centred on York, was being slowly re-formed and pushed ahead by the kings of Wessex, towards a unified English state. The ambitions of the Scottish rulers were focused on Lothian and the territory to the south, known as Bernicia; and also on Cumbria, which had been at different times part of, or a sub-kingdom of, Strathclyde. Had their policies been wholly successful, the Scottish border might now run from the Humber to Morecambe Bay. Northumberland was, however, conquered from the Danes by Athelstan of England, who in 937 went on to lead his army to a great victory over the Scots and their Norse allies at Brunanburh, a site now unknown. Better relations followed, and, in 954, Cumberland was ceded to the Scottish king, Malcolm I. In the same year, after a siege, the Scots took the rock of Din Eiddyn in Lothian from its Anglian garrison. Twenty-two years later, Lothian, which had also been claimed by Athelstan, was formally ceded to King Kenneth II. In both these cases, the English king would have retained an overlordship on the provinces, but the Scots still pressed their claim on Bernicia. In 1006, a Scottish army was soundly defeated outside Durham, but in 1018, with England part of King Cnut's Danish empire, the Scots won a battle at Carham, on the Tweed, after which Lothian was permanently integrated into the Scottish kingdom.

On the death of Malcolm II, King of Scots, in 1034, his grandson Duncan, King of Strathclyde, assumed the kingship of Scots. In previous generations, Strathclyde would then have been given a new sub-king, but none was installed. Instead, there was a single kingship, stretching from Moray to the southern edge of Cumberland. It was around this time that the name of Scotland (an Anglian term) came into use, for a country previously known as Alba or Scotia. But both the old names really meant the country north of Forth. There was little centralised control and great power still resided with the regional lords – known in the former Pictland as mormaers ('great stewards') – particularly the Mormaer of Moray. Irish chronicles of the time frequently referred to the Moray ruler as a *ri*, or king. The ruling families of this province pursued their own turbulent course. To the Kings of Scots, they were at times a useful buffer against the ever-present threat of Norse invasion, but they were also a permanent threat and challenge to the MacAlpin dynasty.

CHAPTER THREE

From the Formation of Scotland to the Collapse of the Kingdom, 1034–1290

The Moray challenge came to a head in the reign of Duncan. Often seen as a kind of personal struggle between Macbeth, Mormaer of Moray, and the king, it is perhaps better viewed in the context of a division that pulled Scottish thought and policy in two directions all through the middle ages – the north-south divide.

Scotland, just protruding into the circumpolar latitudes, was part of a political and economic region that included the Scandinavian lands, Iceland (recently colonised from the Hebridean Norse kingdom) and the Baltic lands. Norwegian possession of much Scottish territory underlined that involvement. But, quite apart from the Scottish kings' itch to hold Northumberland and the consequent focus on the south, a powerful influence was also exerted by England and the rich countries bordering the southern North Sea and the English Channel. Economically more developed (Scotland at this time had no coinage of its own), more populous, and with no separating sea, England acted as a channel of cultural, linguistic and social influence. As in previous ages, what was new, even it had not originated in England, tended to come to Scotland by way of the south.

Macbeth had resented Duncan's accession to the throne, believing that he had a more respectable claim to the Scottish kingship. His wife was of royal blood, and he himself may have been Duncan's first cousin. Macbeth formed a northern league against Duncan with another first cousin of Duncan's, Thorfinn, Earl of Orkney, Caithness and Sutherland. In 1040, they defeated Duncan's army, Duncan was killed, and Macbeth assumed the kingship. He retained it for 17 years. But the MacAlpin dynasty was not yet at an end. Duncan's son Malcolm, with the support of Siward, Earl of Northumberland, at whose court he had grown up, regained first Lothian and Strathclyde in 1054, and finally defeated and killed Macbeth in his own heartland at Lumphanan in 1057. Macbeth's stepson, Lulach, was briefly installed as a king in Moray, but was killed in a further battle at Eassie in the following year. Although descendants of Lulach (whose mother was a grand-daughter of King Malcolm II) would maintain their claim for centuries, it was an increasingly forlorn one.

Malcolm III, Warrior King

Malcolm III, known in Gaelic as *Ceann Mòr*, which might be 'Great Chief' or just 'Big-head', had two marriages that again illustrate the north-south tension. His first wife was Ingibjorg, widow of the Earl of Orkney, and she produced a son named Duncan. Ingibjorg died some time before 1069 for around then Malcolm married Margaret, sister of Edgar Atheling, who had been heir to Harold, King of England. However, when Harold had died at the battle of Hastings in 1066, the kingship of England had been taken by William, Duke of Normandy, and Edgar and Margaret had become refugees. With wide experience of court and church life in Europe, Margaret personified the southern connection. She set out vigorously to bring the manners of the court and the practice of the church into line with modern European ways. It was in this period that the gradual but steady marginalisation of the Gaelic language and the Gaels' way of life began. A new rift opened within the young nation, a cultural and linguistic one, which would have profound and long-term consequences. Instead of Gaelic, the speech of the court and of government became Anglian, the language that would develop into Lowland Scots.

While his wife relentlessly reformed court and religious life, Malcolm III, a warrior king in the old style, made frequent raids into England. In 1070, this resulted in the appearance of an army led by William I of England, which invaded as far as Abernethy before a settlement was achieved. The fact that Scotland had to resist England, to avoid being absorbed into the English state, and yet could never seriously contemplate the conquest of England was a permanent source of dismay to the Scots, and another factor that shaped national attitudes. Since the adage, 'attack is the best form of defence' was well-known already, the Scots often adopted it. The greed, and urge to extend their power, of successive Scottish kings also played their part. Despite submitting to William, Malcolm III continued to raid into England. In 1092, the new English king, William Rufus, took control of Cumberland, building a stronghold at Carlisle, and Scotland finally lost that southern part of the old Strathclyde kingdom.

Malcolm III had based his court at Dunfermline, where his wife endowed a Benedictine abbey, and Dunfermline was to remain a royal town until the seventeenth century. The old Anglian fort of Din Eiddyn, among the rich plains of Lothian, had been reclaimed as a royal lodge, and it was here that Margaret died, in 1093, a few days after hearing of her husband's death in an ambush at Alnwick in Northumberland. There was no capital of Scotland. The largest town was probably Berwick on Tweed, which was also the country's prime seaport, but towns of any sort were rare and small. Much of the land was still covered by dense forest, with the people living along the coasts, in the glens, straths and valleys, and on the loch-sides. At this time many still lived in the lochs, both inland and sea-lochs, in the wooden platform-dwellings known as crannogs, whose history went far back in time.

Malcolm's Successors

The southern emphasis of Malcolm III's government had clearly caused resentment in the Gaelic north (by now it is likely that the Pictish language had completely gone out of use, and Gaelic was universal, except in the

Norse-ruled areas). Malcolm's brother, Donald Bàn, identified himself with this reaction and hastened to seize power after Malcolm's death. It was the last stand of the Celtic party. William Rufus supported Malcolm's first son, Duncan, in an invasion which pushed Donald Bàn back into the Highlands. But Duncan II's brief kingship ended in his assassination and Donald returned, until another English-backed invasion in 1097 finally deposed him and put his nephew, Edgar, fourth son of Malcolm III, on the throne. Duncan II's son, William, retreated into the Highlands, founding a line of MacWilliam claimants to the throne who would stir up trouble periodically.

Edgar's English name symbolised his English leanings. England was now a Norman kingdom, with the feudal system of administration and economic life largely established. It was a disciplined, effective and stable system, backed up by laws and written charters, and the rulers of Scotland were keen to emulate it. Although it had been unified for more than 60 years, the Scottish state was still a somewhat ramshackle one, incorporating the traditions, laws and customs of provinces that had recently been virtual kingdoms themselves and still saw their loyalties in local terms. A system that placed everyone in a clear succession of duty and loyalty in direct line to the king must have seemed immensely desirable. Edgar and his successors would try hard to implement it, but with only limited success.

At this time the organs of government were minimal, and concerned mainly with the provision and protection of the royal household. Written records were kept by abbeys and priories, but these were sparse documents. Literacy was the preserve of churchmen and a very few of the nobility. It was a society in which the ancient oral tradition remained strong and vital, not only in the preservation of story and legend, but in the keeping of historical information. The *seannachaidh,* or historian, was an important functionary at the court of any mormaer or territorial lord. The occupants of the land, tillers of the soil, cow-herds, fishers, foresters, and their women-folk, under their headmen, chieftains and chiefs, lived where their ancestors had always lived, or sometimes where their ancestors had claimed the ground by right of the sword. They had no charters. Their duties to chief and king, of 'Scottish service' in battle, and of the time-honoured 'cain and conveth', provision of food and hospitality, were enshrined in ancient practice. The *toiseach,* or chief, measured his wealth in men and cows. Tribal organisation underlay the laws, which were administered by a cadre of lawmen in each region. Feuds were frequent and bloody, and recognised as part of the way of life. For a king to impose an alien system upon this long-entrenched society was a major struggle. But there were ways and means.

First of all, the king was a great magnate in his own right. He had more fighting men at his disposal than any one of the regional lords (at this time adopting the title of earl rather than mormaer) and could also, by diplomacy, exploit the rivalry that existed between different earls. He could use the device of marriage to extend his own control, by marrying a son to an heiress-daughter, or a daughter to an earl-to-be. His prestige far exceeded that of anyone else, though he was required to maintain it by being a successful war-leader and by generous hospitality and gifts. However tenuous his machinery of government was, it was greater than any other magnate's. Alexander I had a chancellor, a constable and a chamberlain, positions which would eventually become hereditary.

Finally, the king could expect to have the support of the richest and most intelligent organisation in the country, and one that had a well-established network not only nationally but internationally – this was the church. Following the reforms of Queen Margaret's time and later, the Scottish church was well-integrated into the Roman organisation. The sons and successors of Malcolm III would be faithful patrons of the church, and be well-rewarded by it.

Edgar, Alexander I, and especially David I, successive kings over 56 years, applied all these methods. Lordships were carved out, or given, to incoming Norman knights. These men often came from the English estates which the Scots kings had gained by marriage to English princesses. Most of the newcomers were installed south of the Forth, though David I also planted Norman or Breton lordships in the troublesome province of Moray. Three new elements confirmed the new dispensation: the castle, the burgh and the sheriff. The castle, on its mound, provided a strong-point for control of its area. The burgh, often growing up in the security of the castle, provided the supplies and skills the castle needed, as well as a market-place. The sheriff applied, not the law of the tribe, but the law of the king; he was a royal agent, dependent on the king, and he worked by charter, not by custom or tradition.

In the reign of Edgar, the Norwegian occupation of the Western Isles was acknowledged by their cession to the Norwegian king, Magnus III ('Bareleg'). This did not prevent Edgar's successors from trying to reclaim territory held by the Norsemen. Royal rule during the twelfth and thirteenth centuries was usually both determined and strong, and, it seems likely, this was not unwelcome to the people. A nineteenth-century historian of medieval Scotland, R. W. Cochran-Patrick, made the point, on the crucial topic of agriculture: 'reviewing the whole history of agriculture from the dawn of authentic record to the Union, the most prosperous times were undoubtedly the reigns of Alexander II and III.' Governments which ensure the basic prosperity of a country are normally well-regarded by the people, at least by the people who share in the resultant prosperity. Scotland in those times was not a wholly free nation. The old practice of slave-raiding and slave-using was still known, and between the slave and the freeman there was a class of serfs who were essentially the property of their employer and had very little of any sort of freedom. Royal government, with the aid of the church, was the unquestioned form of rule, and any changes in its style or practice came not from pressure from the populace, but by emulation of foreign practice and the self-preserving adaptation of a small ruling group to gradually changing circumstances.

Economic and Social Developments

Fortunate in the stability and long reigns of its dynasty, Scotland shared in a general increase in European trade and prosperity. In the time of David I, a coinage, based on the English model, was introduced. The growth of market and manufacturing centres was fostered by the development of the burgh – a small town whose charter, given by the king (royal burgh) or the local lord (burgh of barony) conferred certain trading rights, and perhaps a monopoly in the making of certain goods. Such rights were of course paid for, through taxes, rents and customs duties, and assured a steady income to the royal government. The four largest burghs in particular, Berwick, Roxburgh, Edinburgh and Stirling, provided themselves with an organisation, the Court of the Four Burghs, to define, protect and enhance burgh rights. The development of towns, though limited in its geographical extent – vast areas in the Highlands, Islands and Galloway had none – helped to build a settled pattern of government. Places like Inverness, or Ayr, far from any other town, but accessible by sea, became the seat of a royal castle and a sheriffdom, marking the king's dominion. Their inhabitants were composed more of English or Scots speakers and even foreigners – English and Flemish traders – than of Gaelic-speaking locals, and the right of residence in the towns was closely controlled.

Another important factor in national life, both economic and social, was the foundation of the monasteries. This did not represent a continuation of the Celtic tradition, in which secular monks, the *Ceile Dei* or 'servants of God' (Culdees) had maintained lives both inside and outside such institutions as St Andrews Cathedral. The new-order monasticism of Europe was imported, with Cistercians at Melrose, Dundrennan, Newbattle and other places, Augustinians at Scone, Holyrood and Jedburgh, and Tironensians at Kelso. The abbeys and priories were endowed with extensive lands and they became centres not only of agricultural activity and improvement, but of fish-farming and trapping, and, not least, of education and learning. The ample new architectural styles developed in Europe – Romanesque, followed by early Gothic – were brought to Scotland by professional masons and craftsmen, resulting in buildings much larger and more imposing than anything seen before. Alexander I also began the establishment of bishoprics, dividing the country into ecclesiastical provinces.

The setting-up of Scottish dioceses resulted in furious controversy within the church during the twelfth century. Three English ecclesiastics, the Archbishops of Canterbury and York, and the Bishop of Durham, all claimed metropolitan authority over the church in Scotland. This was stoutly resisted by the Scots, partly through historical awareness of their continuous Christian tradition when the Anglo-Saxons were pagans, and partly for political reasons at a time when state and church were closely integrated. The dispute was not resolved until 1192, when the Pope, appealed to by both sides, made the Scottish church a 'special daughter' of Rome. At this time the western and northern isles remained part of the far-flung Norwegian diocese of Trondheim.

The Struggle for Northumberland

Scotland had evolved the structures and symbols of a kingdom, but this was not to prevent the neighbouring English kings taking a close and often possessive interest in Scottish affairs, whenever their own troubles allowed it. Scottish kings could return the compliment. The obsessive interest in gaining Northumberland led to much warfare and despoiling, and helped considerably to define the identities of Scots and English along the border. But kingdoms at the time were not nation-states, and the property-owners of Scotland might hold large estates in England, and vice-versa, without troubling themselves over questions of 'nationality'. Self-interest determined the issue. When David I invaded Northumberland in 1138, two of his greatest magnates, both of immigrant Norman families, fought against him. They were Robert de Bruis and John de Balliol, both names to become familiar in later times, and both held land in England as well as Scotland. David I himself was also Earl of Huntingdon, and in that capacity did homage to the English king. He succeeded for a short time in achieving the possession of Northumberland for his family. His son became its earl. But in 1157

Henry II of England prevailed upon David's successor as king, his grandson Malcolm IV, to give up his rights to the earldom. Northumbria was to become an English domain.

When King William I, Malcolm's brother, succeeded to the throne in 1165, his main aim was the recovery of Northumberland and to this end he instigated border wars. In 1174, he was caught in a surprise attack at Alnwick and taken prisoner. To obtain his release he was forced to submit to the English king as his overlord. The subordination of the Scottish king lasted until 1189. In this year, the Quitclaim (deed of release) of Canterbury was agreed, by which the full Scottish sovereignty was restored for a payment of 10,000 merks. The money went into the war-chest of the new English king, Richard I, who was preparing to take part in the Third Crusade. William I's humiliation was forgotten by neither side. Although in the reigns of Alexander II and Alexander III, relations with England were often friendly, the kings' advisers had to be constantly on the watch for English efforts to re-assert their 15-year feudal superiority. When Alexander III, at the age of 10, was married to Henry III's daughter, Margaret, he paid homage to his father-in-law for his English lands, but was well-prepared to avoid the duly-made attempt to include with that the kingdom of Scotland.

The Western Isles
In the course of the thirteenth century, the vigour of the Scottish kingdom, and its proximity to the

Norwegian-held territories of the northern mainland and the Western Isles, resulted in a steady process of 'scottification' there. From the ninth century, the Hebrides were home to a hybrid people, the Gall-Gaels (their name perpetuated in Galloway), of Norse and Gaelic stock, but Gaelic-speaking. Unruly and piratical, they were no more obedient to the Norwegian kings, or the Hebridean kings of the Isle of Man, than they were to the Scottish king. Norwegian control and influence were weakening. In 1242, Alexander II's offer to buy the Hebrides from Norway was refused; seven years later he died on campaign there. An effort was made in the autumn of 1263, by Haakon IV of Norway, to reinstate Norwegian control, but a minor defeat at Largs, a major defeat by the weather, and his own death that winter, combined to frustrate the initiative. In the summer of 1266, it was agreed that Scotland would hold dominion over the Western Isles and the Isle of Man, for a payment of 4,000 merks and an annual rental of a hundred pounds a year. A diplomatic marriage between Princess Margaret, daughter of Alexander III, and King Eric II of Norway, later consummated the deal.

End of a Dynasty

In 1266, Alexander III had been king for 17 years. He had acceded at the age of eight and, for the first time, the country saw the often-to-be-repeated scheming and manoeuvring of ambitious barons to control a child-monarch. Primogeniture was established by now, and the kingship was not contested. But two strong families, the Comyns and Durwards, with their allies, struggled to rule in the child's name, with his father-in-law, Henry III of Enland, closely involved. This was when the pattern of appeal to the power of England began, which would be followed, either openly or covertly, by many disappointed Scottish grandees in generations to come. It was only when Walter Comyn, head of that faction, fortuitously died in 1258 that Alexander began to exert his own personal power at the age of 17.

In 1286, Alexander III was killed when his horse stumbled on the cliffs at Kinghorn, in Fife. His only direct heir was his infant grand-daughter, Margaret, the 'Maid of Norway'. She was duly proclaimed Queen of Scots, and a Council of Guardians from among the lords and bishops was appointed to rule on her behalf. The collapse of the kingdom happened, not on the death of Alexander, but on the death of the child-queen, which happened four years later in 1290, in Orkney, on her way to be crowned at Scone.

Chapter Four

The Wars of Independence and the First Stewarts, 1290–1424

There was no obvious heir to the throne of Scotland on the death of the young Queen Margaret. A highly interested party was Edward I of England, whose son, Edward of Caernarvon, had been meant to marry the young queen. This was a provision of the Scottish-English Treaty of Birgham, made in 1290, which also provided for the continued independence of Scotland. The subsequent behaviour of Edward makes his intention to honour this clause questionable at the least. But events never put this to the test.

John Balliol

It was a situation of great uncertainty. A medieval city-state could flourish without a hereditary sovereign; a country divided into earldoms and lordships could not. Robert Bruce, Lord of Annandale, put himself forward for the crown, and led an army to Perth. He sought Edward's support, as did the Bishop of St Andrews, who feared that civil war would break out.

Edward took the opportunity not only to act as arbiter in the 'competition' that ensued among 13 claimants for the kingship, but formally renewed the English claim to overlordship of Scotland and ensured that they all swore, if elected, to acknowledge him as their feudal overlord.

By close examination of ancestry, the kingship was awarded to John Balliol in November 1292. Edward's action had turned the trophy into something of a poisoned chalice, however. The Scottish expectation was that the new king would maintain the rights and status – and prosperity – of Scotland. The English expectation was that the new king was a sort of provincial governor in the Plantagenet empire which extended into Wales and France. Edward attempted to summon Scots as part of his feudal host to make war in Gascony. Balliol's council denied his right to do this, and made an alliance with Edward's French opponents.

In 1296, Edward I invaded Scotland, won an easy victory at Dunbar, and proceeded to depose King John and take him away as a prisoner. The Scottish barons surrendered; their vows of loyalty to Edward are still preserved in their seals dangling from the 35 parchment sheets known as the 'Ragman Rolls'. To underline his control, Edward I had the royal regalia of Scotland removed, together with most official records. Also removed was the Stone of Destiny, brought by the Scots to Iona in the sixth century, and later transferred to Scone Abbey. On it the kings of the Scots had been crowned since ancient times.

Wallace and Moray – Guardians of Scotland
As forcibly as the English king denied the entity of a

Scottish kingdom, so the supporters of that kingdom upheld it. Resistance became manifest, not among the great nobles, but among the lesser gentry. It coalesced around two young men, William Wallace in the south-west and Andrew Moray in the north-east. Both were well-connected in their regions. Both might have lived peaceably as country landowners, but they took up arms against the occupation of Scotland by English forces, and the exploitation and ill-treatment of Scots by Edward's governors, notably Ormsby, his Justiciar, and Cressingham, his Lord Treasurer.

Another vital source of resistance lay in the church. The Scottish bishops had their own reasons for opposing English rule, not least their wish to preserve their own church's independence, and some of them were to play notable parts in the wars of independence which now began. Chief among them was Robert Wishart, Bishop of Glasgow, who was a supporter of Wallace, and whose contacts included James, the hereditary Steward of Scotland, who was opposed to Edward but keeping a safely low profile.

By the end of 1297, Andrew Moray controlled all Scotland north of the Tay, in the name of the imprisoned King John. Wallace and Sir James Douglas were leading anti-English raids in the south. In June 1297, the young Robert Bruce, grandson of the Bruce who had failed to become king in 1290, was involved, with the Steward, in an ignominious defeat by the English at Irvine. Moray and Wallace, now named Guardians of Scotland in a new context, united their forces and defeated an English army at Stirling Bridge in September of that year. The conquest of armoured knights by foot-soldiers was unprecedented and news of it raced round Europe. Moray died of his wounds shortly after the battle, but Wallace went on to capture Berwick and make raids on Northumberland. He became Sir William Wallace and sole Guardian of Scotland.

Preparations for war went on, though Wallace preferred the guerrilla type of warfare to pitched battles. Nevertheless in July 1298, he was manoeuvred into a full battle against Edward's army at Falkirk. The Scots were defeated and Wallace went into hiding in the forests. New Guardians were installed: Robert Bruce (for a time), John Comyn, and William Lamberton, the new Bishop of St Andrews. Scottish delegations went to Paris and Rome to enlist help in the freeing of John Balliol. For a time, this seemed likely, but it did not happen, and intermittent war resumed.

In 1303, Edward I returned to Scotland with a large army and through a long, bitter winter campaign, again enforced the submission of the Scottish nobles. One by one the castles were restored to English control – the last to fall was Stirling in July 1304. Wallace continued his guerrilla campaigns until in August 1305 he was captured, sent to England for trial, and executed as a traitor against King Edward, to whom he had never sworn loyalty. His brutal execution, intended both as revenge and deterrent, would become a mainspring of Scottish patriotic feeling for centuries to come.

Robert I, 'The Bruce'

Following his brief guardianship, Robert Bruce had renewed his loyalty to Edward I. Now in March 1306, he asserted the Bruce claim to the throne in the most flamboyant way possible, by arranging for his own coronation as King of Scots, at Scone. He could hardly have managed it in worse circumstances. The previous month, he had met with John Comyn in the Greyfriars' Church in Dumfries – perhaps hoping to clear the way for a bid for the throne. However, the meeting had ended with Bruce stabbing Comyn to death – an act that not only risked his excommunication but which set the great Comyn faction permanently against him. Despite this sacrilege, Bishop Lamberton officiated at Bruce's coronation and Bishop Wishart found him suitable robes.

Soon afterwards, Bruce was on the run. In June 1306, his army was defeated by an English force at Methven, near Perth, and a short time later his depleted force was beaten again by MacDougall of Argyll, a Comyn ally, at Tyndrum. The new king had to flee the mainland for Rathlin Island, off the Antrim coast, and for four months nothing was heard of him. He may even have gone to Norway. His queen was a prisoner, and those who had fought for him were executed as traitors. Bishop Lamberton and Bishop Wishart were sent to England in chains.

The long, slow, painful struggle to establish his kingship lasted for seven years. Although he kept the support of the steward, the bishops, and the numerous barons and Highland chiefs, the critical factor was the support of the Scottish people. Though Bruce, like others, could employ brutal sanctions to force men into his army, there was increasing popular consent for his kingship, despite the fact that King John was still alive and a prisoner in France. Ten years of struggle had showed that the Scots would not give up their concept of a kingdom. In some ways that concept was unlike any other in Europe. The Declaration of Arbroath, in 1320, would make that clear by spelling out the fact that if the king did not defend the liberties of the people, he would be replaced by someone who would.

The death of Edward I in 1307 eased the situation. From 1308, Robert I was able to govern much of Scotland and by 1309 he was able to hold a parliament at St Andrews. By 1313, only one castle remained in English hands, that of Stirling. By a chivalric arrangement, it was agreed that the castle would be given a year's respite, after which it would surrender if an English army had not appeared to relieve it. The challenge to England was not to be ignored. With a few days to spare, Edward II, with an army some 20,000 strong, arrived outside Stirling. Not without severe misgivings, Robert I mustered his smaller force to meet it. His success had been based on what the poet-chronicler, William Barbour, called 'Scottis weir' (war) – raids, ambushes, sudden attacks – certainly not a pitched battle against some of the heaviest cavalry in Europe. He had deliberately avoided such a battle when Edward II invaded Scotland in 1310–11. In the end, the battle of Bannockburn, in June 1314, was a decisive victory for the Scots, to rank with the ancient triumph of the Picts at Dunnichen. Robert I's position as king and leader of the Scots was ensured, and the way was prepared for the eventual English recognition of his title, and of Scottish independence, in 1328.

The Effects of the Wars

The real impact of the period from 1296 to 1314 on Scottish life is hard to assess. Much of the country's wealth was drained out by English taxation and exploitation in the earlier part of the period. Later, the disruption of war, the destruction of castles and towns, the pressing of able-bodied men into the army, the cost of equipping and maintaining the army, the loss of rents and payments in kind, must all have severely damaged the economy. One of Bruce's reasons for holding parliaments was in order to bring the burghs, with their financial resources, into his plans. But many of them were impoverished. Berwick, the main port, sacked by Edward I in 1296, and vulnerably located on the border, was in decline. On the other hand, after 1314, Scottish raids into northern England went on regularly for years and much wealth was drawn back into Scotland as spoils and booty. It seems likely that plague and warfare later in the fourteenth century had a more drastic and lasting effect than the wars of independence.

Robert I died in 1329. He had been an exemplary king for his time. Quite apart from restoring the integrity of the kingdom, his government had striven to maintain, or repair, the country's economy, with legislation on aspects of agriculture and fishing. His Gaelic connections, and the involvement of Highlanders and Islanders in the Bannockburn victory, helped to recreate the sense of a single nation among his divided people. (In 1307, though, he had carried out the brutal 'herschip', or harrying, of Buchan, rooting out the Gaelic-speaking Comyn adherents and transforming the province into a Scots-speaking zone.) Many people old enough to remember the days before 1292 might have thought that the good times had returned again, with a stable kingdom, and a promising future. They would have been wrong.

A New War of Independence

The fourteenth century was to be a painful and difficult time for the Scottish people, as for most other Europeans. Bruce's achievement had not seen the end of war with England, or of disputes over the throne. Edward Balliol, the (somewhat unfortunately named) son of the now-dead King John, obtained English backing for an attempt to seize the kingship in 1332. Another boy-king was on the throne, David II, son of Robert I; the Balliol threat was serious enough for him and his equally juvenile bride, Joan of England, to be sent to France for their safety, in 1334.

In 1335, Edward III of England invaded Scotland and his army made its way as far north as Elgin. Great tracts of the Scottish borders were placed under English rule. Once again the always-small but never quite dead ganglion of government at the heart of the Scottish state nominated guardians of the realm; once again a resistance movement arose to confront the armed might of the great neighbour-state. Edward Balliol, despite a victory by his supporters at Dupplin Moor in Fife against the guardians' army, never found general acceptance as king. It was 1341 before David II returned from France, full of ambitious chivalric notions that his father, in his maturity, would have deplored. Five years later, he led an invasion into England and was captured at the battle of Halidon Hill. The Steward of Scotland assumed control of the government. Apart from one temporary parole visit, it was 11 years before David II returned. During that time the Black Death made its silent, devastating way through Scotland, causing far more mortality than any war.

Death Crosses the Border

At first the Scots had felt secure; they had even mocked at the depredations of plague in England in 1347 and 1348. It seemed as if the plague would not cross the border. When it inevitably did, its effects were catastrophic. The contemporary chronicler, John of Fordun, wrote: 'To such a pitch did the plague wreak its cruel spite, that nearly a third of mankind were thereby made to pay the debt of nature ... Men shrank from it so much that, through fear of contagion, sons, fleeing as from the face of leprosy or from an adder, durst not go and see their parents in the throes of death.' Fordun's estimate of a third of the population dying may have been too high, though other sources quote the same proportion, but the numbers of dead were terrifyingly large. The poor, that is the majority of the population, living in close-packed hut-like dwellings lacking air and light, were more at risk than those who dwelt in castles.

Most historians of Scotland, being more interested in battles and politics, have deplored and quickly passed over the effects of the plague. But, as Philip Ziegler, historian of the Black Death, wrote, with a degree of understatement: 'One third of a country's population cannot be eliminated over a period of some two and a half years without considerable dislocation to its economy and social structure.' He was referring to England, but exactly the same could be said for Scotland.

T. Bedford Franklin's *History of Scottish Farming* records how 1350, the year of the Black Death, marked the end of the land-clearing and agricultural activities of Coupar Angus Abbey. The monks were no longer numerous enough to man their granges, and became landlords, renting out their lands, rather than farmers. So many people died that agricultural labourers, the majority of workers, were suddenly at a premium and their wages went up. Any lingering instances of serfdom (which seems to have died out in Scotland earlier than in most European countries) were eliminated by the shortage of labour induced by the plague. But much land went untilled because of the deaths of ploughmen and husbandmen (managers).

The combined effects of plague, invasion and civil strife showed themselves in widespread destitution and misery. Once-flourishing towns, such as Perth, were reduced to shadow-places. The countryside was bare of crops and animals over wide areas. Human desperation led to reported cases of cannibalism. Among the repercussions was a more secular spirit among the people. Religious faith took a battering, and there were fewer recruits to monastic life in the post-plague years. As a result, there was a marked deterioration in the quality of churchmen. Retaining its lands and its potential wealth, the church began to be more a source of income for the nobility than a spiritual body which could claim to represent the whole community of the realm. The teinds, or tithes, exacted from every farm, went in the main to swell the riches of abbeys and abbots, while parish priests were poorly paid and often only semi-literate.

A New Dynasty – the First Stewart

David II's kingdom had to find the sum of 100,000 merks to ransom him from England. To raise so huge a sum was impossible without the co-operation of the towns, and from his return in 1357, a Scottish parliament became a more important feature in national life, combining the 'Three Estates' of nobility, clergy and the burgesses (royal burgh commissioners). During David's exile, the kingdom had been administered by his nephew, Robert the Steward (actually eight years older than his royal uncle), in a lax and easy-going way. The king attempted to bring in some reforms to encourage trade and reform the treasury; but he also began the ultimately disastrous policy of devaluing the currency. The Scots silver penny, increasingly mixed with alloy, sank dramatically in value.

Relations between king and steward were poisonous, with plots and counter-plots and occasional efforts at rebellion. But Robert, grandson of Robert I through his mother, was also the heir-presumptive to the throne, and David, despite two marriages, had produced no legitimate heir. When he died in 1371, the Steward became King Robert II, and founder of the Stewart dynasty.

Despite his earlier caretaker role, Robert II was in spirit more of a baron than a king. His mental horizon was bounded by considerations of property and family. Already during the childhood of Alexander III, the country had seen how baronial self-interest would stick at nothing, including a sell-out to England, in order to gain or keep power. It needed a strong kingship to keep the nobility in line, and this was not something the first Stewart kings could provide. In the following centuries, their descendants paid the price, as did the mass of the inhabitants of a country burdened with a caste of arrogant, boorish, self-satisfied, ignorant and greedy earls and lords, whose feuds, wars and treacheries consumed much of the national wealth and life. A strong king was not a good thing in the eyes of the Scots nobles.

The Clans

In the west, the Macdonald Lords of the Isles ruled a semi-independent territory from Finlaggan on Islay. The vision of their galleys skimming the Hebridean seas, and the Gaelic speech and culture of their court have given them a romantic tinge to some modern writers. In the south, the Douglases, a family that had prospered and expanded since the time of Robert I, when the 'good Sir James Douglas' was one of his chief lieutenants, saw themselves as a rival dynasty to the Stewarts; indeed an Earl of Douglas had made a bid for the throne before Robert II was crowned. No part of the country was without its lord, whether his estate was a large regality (in which he enjoyed virtually unlimited power) or a more modest holding spread around a narrow stone tower house. Territories and boundaries were always in dispute, and most disputes led to bloodshed. By this time, many lords held charters or written titles to their lands, but many did not. Particularly in the Highlands, communities more or less loosely organised as clans or clan groups occupied areas of glen and mountainside which had been their homes from times long before Norman ways were imported. Gaelic *clann* means 'children' and they traced their ancestry back to a common ancestor and often further back from him to some hero of ancient legend. A large clan was a complex organisation, often with scattered patches of territory; and with sub-clans or septs who had originally fulfilled hereditary roles within the system, in a continuing though much-altered and attenuated version of the old tribal organisation. Thus families such as the MacMhuirichs were hereditary bards, and kept a great store of bardic verse, both oral and (later) written down; the Beatons likewise maintained a medical tradition over the centuries.

Wars, Truces and Uneasy Peace

For a large part of the fourteenth century, King Edward III of England was a serious threat to Scottish independence. He had tried to have a son of his installed as heir to David II. After Edward's death in 1377, the Scots were able to reclaim most of the land he had annexed, but relations with England remained tense, through a series of short wars, truces and periods of uneasy peace.

During this long period, the alliance between Scotland and France was frequently renewed and invoked. In 1385, a French force landed to assist in the defence of Scotland against the forces of John of Gaunt and Richard II, though it achieved little.

During one period of truce, Donald Macdonald, future Lord of the Isles, was given a safe-conduct to attend classes at Oxford University. But, of the young Scots who received a higher education, most went to Italian or French universities. The French link offered access to a more advanced civilisation than Scotland possessed. In the church and within the nobility there were men of ability and cosmopolitan interests who were capable of looking beyond the frontiers of their own turbulent and somewhat backward nation and trying to import elements of European progress.

The weak rule of Robert II resulted in a crisis in December 1388 when he appears to have given up his powers; and his second son, Robert, Earl of Fife, was named Guardian. This man, later created Duke of Albany, was never king but was effectively the ruler of Scotland for 32 years until his death in 1420, whilst his father (till 1390) and his elder brother, Robert III (till 1406), were titular kings, and his nephew James I was a prisoner in England. Albany was almost certainly responsible for arranging the death of Robert III's elder son David, Duke of Rothesay, in 1402. He was a strong man, but still a baron among barons, and the Highlands slipped further out of royal control.

In a notorious episode, one of the many sons of Robert II, Alexander Stewart, titular Justiciar of the North but better known as the 'Wolf of Badenoch', burned down Elgin Cathedral and much of the town in the course of a feud with the Bishop of Moray. The culture of revenge and the blood-feud ran unchecked, even encouraged, as in the royally sponsored and supervised clan battle at Perth in September 1396.

The most spectacular case of baronial war was in 1411. A dispute between Donald Macdonald, Lord of the Isles, and Governor Albany over the vacant earldom of Ross resulted in a full-scale battle at Harlaw, near Aberdeen, between armies led by the Stewart Earl of Mar and Donald – himself half Stewart through his mother. The fight was inconclusive, but it was Donald who retreated.

One of Robert III's few known initiatives was to send his younger son James to France, for his own security, in 1406. Even this was a failure, as the boy was captured by an English ship and taken to London, where he was kept prisoner. Warfare had again broken out with England, and a defeat at Homildon Hill in 1402 had resulted in Albany's son, Murdoch, also being made an

English captive. Murdoch was eventually ransomed in 1416, while James remained in captivity until 1424.

Life in the Burghs

Set against this depressing background of Scottish life around the turn of the fourteenth century is a more progressive picture of life in the burghs. Local government was often vigorous, and the trading and manufacturing of the towns were encouraged by local magnates, who were keen to purchase foreign goods, whether Ferrara swords or Flemish tapestries. The trade in wine was a long-established one by now. The burghs kept money in circulation, and could exert economic pressure to have their privileges increased. In 1410, the country's first university was founded at St Andrews by Bishop Wardlaw.

At this time, the Catholic church was caught in the Great Schism, with rival Popes based in Rome and Avignon. England favoured Rome; Scotland, predictably, followed France and supported the Avignon Pope. The need to avoid pro-Roman institutions may have encouraged the founding of the new university. But there was also an emerging need to defend Catholic orthodoxy and tradition against the first murmurings for reform. 'Lollardy' was the name given to a movement, originating at Oxford, whose adherents (Lollards) objected to the trade in indulgences, the fashion for pilgrimages and clerical celibacy, among other things. In 1406, an English Lollard was burned at the stake in Perth for heresy.

James I Returns to Scotland

Albany's long dominance ended with his death in 1420. Murdoch succeeded him as duke and governor of Scotland, in the name of the still-imprisoned James I, and lived a life of hunts and jousts, with no effort to exert control despite his alleged ambition for the throne.

Meanwhile, things were moving in England, where James I had won the support of the powerful Beaufort family – Joan Beaufort was to be his queen. Three years of negotiation ended in the fixing of a thinly disguised ransom – as the cost of his 'education' – and 21 Scots nobles went to England as hostages pending its payment. On 5 April 1424, James I, aged thirty, returned to the country he had left as a boy of eleven.

CHAPTER FIVE

A European Nation-State,
1424–1513

James was well-informed about Scotland, its leading
citizens and its current condition. At that time, for its
inhabitants, Europe effectively constituted the world.
America, most of Africa, and Australia were unknown.
Tenuous trade links for silks and spices stretched east
and south-east into Asia, and a tiny proportion of these
goods found their way to Scotland.

The Scots' world was a North Sea one, a busy network
of trading links to Norway, Sweden, the Low Countries,
the Hanseatic ports, and into the Baltic. Salted herrings,
dried cod and coarse wool were the main exports; timber,
tar and iron ore were the import commodities. Other
links ran south-west to Bordeaux and Spain, chiefly for
wine. In 1407, Scottish merchants had achieved a long-
held ambition by establishing a 'staple' port at Bruges
in Flanders, an import-export centre under their own
management, free of tolls and unimpeded by English
rivalry.

The Scottish trading towns, all on the east coast,
from Inverness to Dunbar (Berwick being at the time
in English possession), wanted stability and security.
They saw little of these in their own hinterland. Despite
the lax rule of James's predecessors, the machinery of
government still existed, in the form of a royal council,

a parliament and sheriffdoms. The church was a major power, owning much of the country's best farmland and enjoying a vast income from rents and teinds (tithes), even if much of this was re-absorbed by aristocratic prelates. The Great Schism ended in 1418, with Scotland the last state in Europe to accept the single Rome-based papacy of Martin V. One of the Schism's results had been to give the country its first cardinal, Walter Wardlaw, appointed by Avignon in 1383.

Half the population spoke Scots, and half spoke Gaelic, by then beginning to be referred to as Erse, or Irish. Gaelic was the speech of the Highlands and Islands, although the greater chiefs and lords were bilingual. Most of them maintained a traditional Gaelic culture, shared with Ireland. Poets and other professionals travelled freely between the courts of Scottish and Irish chiefs, and the main bardic schools were at this time in Ireland. The dominant figure was the Lord of the Isles, who issued his own charters and was a very theoretical subject of the Scottish king. At the height of their power, the Macdonald Lords of the Isles controlled much of the northern mainland. In the central Highlands and the north-east, earls of Stewart descent ruled like petty kings.

James I and Social Reform

James I's achievement was to restore strength and authority to the role of the king. His supporters in this were the burghs, the professional churchmen and the smaller landowners – all those with a vested interest in stable government as the only way of hemming in the earls. From among the country lairds he chose most of his key officers. Parliament was also an important tool for reform. Never had there been such a flow of law-making, and James also sought to abolish the many archaic legal privileges which some magnates possessed and used for the benefit of themselves and their retainers. Efforts to establish the rule of law throughout the land were hampered by the fact that there was as yet no professional judiciary. Local landowners dispensed justice, and the royal instruction, that it was to be administered equally to rich and poor, shows that such was not actually the case.

In 1428, the king made an expedition into the Highlands, summoning the leading men to a gathering at Inverness, and clapping them all into custody. Some were hanged, some were exiled. The main aim was to force the submission of Alexander, Lord of the Isles. Alexander submitted, escaped, was forced to submit again, but the entrenched and ramified power of the Macdonalds was too great for a quick campaign to succeed. In 1431, a royal army was defeated at Inverlochy by a force led by Alexander's cousin, Donald Balloch. The Highlands remained untamed.

Round the edges of the Highlands, royal policy seemed more successful. Great earldoms such as Buchan, Fife, Lennox and Mar were brought under control of the crown. How far an acquisitive greed on the king's part lay behind this is impossible to tell – no king of Scotland ever felt adequately well-off – but the result was a ground swell of resentment and outrage among the country's leading families. This was especially true of James's own kindred, the Stewarts. Happy enough to see the country divided out among the family, they were enraged at James's use of royal power and quasi-legal pretexts to obtain vast domains for himself. On 21 February 1437, his half-uncle, the Earl of Atholl, with a small band of supporters, burst in on the king at the Blackfriars' monastery in Perth and stabbed him to death.

The Struggle for Power – Crichton and Livingston

The conspirators' hope for a restitution of the old Stewart ways, possibly by Atholl becoming king, was very speedily dashed. Arrest and execution followed, and the six-year-old son of James I was crowned at Holyrood as James II. Two of his father's appointees, Sir William Crichton, Governor of Edinburgh Castle, and Sir Alexander Livingston, Governor of Stirling Castle, struggled for power by holding the boy-king. Titular governor of the country was Archibald, the 5th Earl of Douglas, head of by far the most powerful family group south of the Highland line. He died in 1439 and the new earl was a boy of seventeen. In those days, when children worked from the age of five or six, and had a life expectancy barely exceeding forty even for the better-off, seventeen was considered mature, and the young earl was incautiously boastful about his military strength and ambition. Crichton, now chancellor, and Livingston united to get rid of any Douglas threat and in November 1440, at the notorious 'Douglas Dinner' in Edinburgh Castle, had the 6th Earl of Douglas and his younger brother dragged away from the dining table and beheaded.

Business in the country went on whilst politics consisted of infighting between the Crichton and Livingston families and their supporters. Allied with the still-powerful Douglases, the Livingstons gained ascendancy. But without great territorial bases, these new governors needed to preserve the systems of taxation and the gathering of customs dues, to ensure an income, and the structures of government were maintained. In those years, the Renaissance was taking place in Europe, trade was expanding, and the Scottish economy also grew. There were diplomatic links with Europe; of James II's six sisters, five married European princes or dukes. Scottish soldiers fought in large numbers in France, on both sides, in the long continuing warfare which eventually pushed the English back to the redoubt of Calais.

The Fall of the Black Douglases
In his late teens, and already married to a French bride, Mary of Gueldres, James, known as 'James of the Fiery Face' because of a red birthmark, began to assume direction of affairs, encouraged perhaps by the ousted Crichton faction. Two Livingstons were executed and the estates the family had acquired were claimed by the crown, while William Crichton was re-appointed as chancellor. The new Earl of Douglas was maintaining a state as great as that of the king and,

when James II made an attempt to reduce his power, the earl successfully resisted it. He was known to have formed a 'band', or agreement for mutual support, with Alexander, Lord of the Isles and Earl of Ross, and the Earl of Crawford, making a trio whose combined power was greater than the king's. In February 1452, invited to Stirling Castle under a pledge of safe conduct, Douglas was confronted by the king. Refusing to back down, the earl was stabbed by James and speedily finished off by the king's attendants.

A kind of intermittent civil war ensued for three years. Many of the nobility stood aside from the king, though parliament – unsurprisingly – acquitted him of murder. Those who supported the king, often minor figures, saw their fortunes rise as he gradually triumphed over the Ross-Crawford factions. They included Colin Campbell, who became Earl of Argyll. In June 1455, in a final battle at Arkinholm, the Douglases were defeated. The earl was already a refugee in England.

Another Boy-King

Ever since the incursions of Edward III of England in the previous century, England had maintained control of a strategic border fortress on the Scottish side, at Roxburgh Castle. James I had failed in an effort to capture it. In 1456, with English politics distracted by the rivalry of York and Lancaster, James II set out to take back Roxburgh Castle. During the siege, a cannon exploded next to him and he was killed. His eldest son, aged eight, was crowned James III at Kelso.

Once again factions formed. The civil wars in England were a test for Scottish diplomacy. The Lancastrians wooed the king, while the Yorkists appealed to the king's enemies, both making promises. Queen Marie, the king's mother, and James Kennedy, Bishop of St Andrews (and another of the many who could call Robert III 'grandfather'), headed the king's council, sometimes in agreement with each other, sometimes not. Kennedy's policy was pro-Lancastrian, and in 1461 Scotland gave refuge to the deposed Henry VI, who returned Berwick on Tweed to Scottish control.

In the following year, a secret treaty was made by Edward IV of England with John, Lord of the Isles, and the exiled Earl of Douglas. Known as the Treaty of Westminster-Ardtornish (the Macdonald fortress on Loch Aline), it provided for the break-up of the kingdom into three parts, one for each signatory. But the two Scottish lords would hold their domains as vassals of the English king. However, although the king's mother died in 1463, and the bishop in 1465, neither of the conspirators could get any purchase on events in Scotland. The government was taken over by two families of the 'new' nobility, the Boyds and the Kennedys.

The Boyd Government

The Boyd government achieved a *coup* in 1468, by arranging the marriage of James III to Margaret, daughter of King Christian I of Denmark. Christian was also King of Norway, and the question of the long-unpaid rental on the Hebrides was an open issue between his government and that of Scotland. Now it was resolved in a way highly satisfactory to Scotland. As part of the marriage settlement, the 'Norway Annual' would be abolished, and its accumulated arrears written off. In addition, a dowry of 60,000 Rhenish florins was to be paid. As Christian could not produce such a sum, first Orkney, then also Shetland were pledged to Scotland until he could find the money. The provisional arrangement soon became a permanent one. On 20 February 1472, the islands were formally annexed to the kingdom of Scotland, restoring the *status quo* of ancient Pictland.

In what was to become an established pattern, James III, at the age of eighteen, violently rid himself of his self-appointed minister-guardians. The Boyd lands, including Bute and Arran, were forfeited to the crown and became the property of the crown prince of Scotland.

The Agricultural Landscape

We know that timber was already being imported at this time. Much of the Scottish landscape was still covered in forest, but it was often inaccessible, or too expensive to extract. The Norwegian trade was based on cutting forests close to the coast. In Scotland, much of the ground close to populated areas was already bare. In Lothian, Lanarkshire and Ayrshire, exposed coal seams or heughs had long been exploited for fuel. Peat moors were dug up. Broom was planted in 'parks' as a fuel and winter fodder supply. A fire was a vital requirement for every house, and foraging for firewood was an essential task. But not a simple one: the resources of the country, down to the rabbit warrens, were minutely identified and parcelled out. Boundaries of land were usually unmarked except by occasional stones, sometimes still standing as 'harestanes', and had to be regularly ridden to ensure no neighbour was encroaching. Fishing and hunting rights were rigorously maintained. James I had arrogated all rights in the mining of gold and silver to the crown.

It was still an almost entirely agrarian society. Out in the countryside, houses were set in random clusters, with the tilled fields spreading away from them. The best ground, or 'infield', was normally that nearest the houses. Parcelled out into strips, it was worked on the 'runrig' system, in which the land was worked in common by all the tenants, with each share normally awarded by lot. The runrigs would be regularly turned and manured. Oats – 'grey oats' rather than the later and more productive white oats – were grown, also barley and wheat, and perhaps peas or beans. Beyond, rising up the hillside, would be the 'outfield', a larger area treated mostly as pasture land, but whose lower areas might be used for crops if demand required it.

Agricultural implements were simple and lightweight – it would be some time before heavy horses were bred for agricultural work. Drainage of the ground was largely left to nature, with the result that much potentially fertile low-lying land was boggy and marshy. In summer,

the cattle were moved to higher grazing, accompanied
by their attendants, who lived rough in shielings (huts)
and did the herding and milking. Little money circulated
and most transactions were done wholly or mainly in
kind. In both Highlands and Lowlands, it was a slow-
changing, tradition-rich society, its life dictated by the
seasons and lived to their rhythm.

Changes tended to be imposed from above, reflecting
the needs, problems, demands and aspirations of the
tiny section of society forming the nobility. As a result,
they were mostly aimed at securing or enhancing the
wealth and status of the owners of the land. There was
a steady trend of encroachment by greater landowners
on the ground occupied by small farmers. Tenancies
were usually for a fixed period of two to five years,
and the leases often included services of various kinds
from military service to unpaid assistance on the
superior's land. Almost invariably, a farm would be
'thirled' (restricted) to a particular mill, owned by or
paying duty to the landowner. Increasingly during the
fifteenth century the custom of 'feuing' land became
commonplace. This meant in effect selling the lease
to the tenant for a cash sum and a low annual rent. It
gave a boost to the landlord's capital, and provided
the tenant with security. The tenant could also sublet.
Many, however, could not raise the initial cash and were
dispossessed by those who could. In some districts,
an older tradition of 'kindly tenants' prevailed; these
were tenants who held their land at a low rent through
some special dispensation, perhaps because of ancestral

links or services. Such arrangements tended to fall apart when the landlord sold out. Large areas in the Highlands continued to be occupied on a basis of 'we have always been here', with its corollary 'and we will fight to remain', but increasingly the onus was being put on those who occupied the land to prove their right to it. At this time the population was probably less than a million, but good land was at a premium everywhere in the country.

The Isolation of James III

In 1475, the existence of the Westminster-Ardtornish treaty between King Edward IV and John, Lord of the Isles, was discovered. James III sent a force to bring John to Edinburgh. Once again a Lord of the Isles was forced to humble himself to the King of Scots, and the earldom of Ross was taken from him. Relations between the king and the territorial barons were not good. They were reactionary backwoodsmen, and he was a modern-minded figure, interested in the new developments in the arts and sciences. The lords despised him and the cultured circle that formed his immediate entourage. Their attitude was shared by the king's brothers, the Duke of Albany and the Earl of Mar. James had them both imprisoned. Albany escaped and fled to England; Mar died in unexplained circumstances.

An unusual diplomatic initiative was tried in this reign when James initiated friendly overtures to England. But traditional attitudes eventually resumed. A coterie of hostile Scots including Albany, Lord Boyd and the Earl of Douglas, lived as clients of the English king, and did their best to suborn their friends and relations still in Scotland.

The existence of an anti-royal party was shown in the vicious scene at Lauder in 1482, when a cabal of nobles seized some of James III's 'familiars' and hanged them from the bridge; their master powerless to intervene. The king was on his way, with his army, to face an English invasion; instead he was put in custody, a truce with England was arranged, and the Duke of Albany returned to Edinburgh in triumph, supported by an English army. On its way home, this army captured Berwick, which has remained in England ever since. Its importance to England was as a strategically placed fortress; its economic importance to Scotland had long since gone. Edinburgh, with its adjacent port of Leith, had become the pre-eminent town by a long way, and its castle was the principal royal prison and treasury. Albany procured himself the title of lieutenant-general, but he and his associates shrank from killing, or even continuing to imprison, the king, and within a year James had regained control of affairs. Albany was forced to resign, was accused of treason, and fled to England. In the following year, he and the Earl of Douglas attempted an invasion, but were defeated at Lochmaben. Albany escaped to France and Douglas was confined in Lindores Abbey where he died in 1488.

James III, perhaps over-confident after surviving these adventures, and still at odds with the 'old' nobility, made a new set of enemies in the border family of Home, who had risen to power after the decline of the Douglases. Within the fortified walls of the other royal castle, Stirling, the king had built a charming small Renaissance-style palace. Here his 16-year-old son, James, Duke of Rothesay, was living in the care of the governor. This official allowed the Homes to take possession of the far from unwilling prince, who accepted the title of governor-elect. James III's main support had always been in the north-east, and he hurried there to raise an army, while his opponents gathered a force in the south. On 11 June 1488, they met at the Sauchie Burn, near Bannockburn. The king's nervous agitation was such that he was advised to leave the battlefield while his troops fought on. Taking refuge in a miller's house by the Bannock Burn, James III was stabbed to death by a mysterious stranger claiming to be a priest.

It is likely that the opposition had hoped for his abdication. The murder – the king's assailant was never found, or revealed – was a grave embarrassment and, whether or not the tale of his iron chain of penance is true, James IV could never live down the means of his premature arrival on the throne.

A Flamboyant Reign

What did the Scots, in the late fifteenth century, expect of their king? Things had moved some way since the Declaration of Arbroath, and the Stewarts were established beyond challenge as the ruling dynasty. But the previous reign had shown that an individual king was not inviolable. Perhaps the chief requirement of the king was to provide a firm and stable rule. The concept of individual rights scarcely existed, but ideas of justice and law did, and it was clear that only through a vigorous kingship could there be certainty that justice and law would be maintained. The next requirement was to defend the integrity of the kingdom. A king was still seen as a war-leader. The third requirement was to personify the prestige of the kingdom. The nation of grey-clad farmers, fishers, miners and artisans, most of them living at a level close to subsistence, did not lack pride in its own existence and history. A king of Scots could be, should be, grand – just as the tribal chief of old was required to be conspicuous in his display and his generosity. But – and here was a distinct Scottish quality – he should not be remote. A bit of the common touch was needed. James IV provided all this, far more effectively than his father.

Government was slowly becoming a more substantial element in national life. Through the fifteenth century a social cadre of administrative families had gradually arisen, of moderate wealth, and owning modest but usually well-situated and fertile estates. Their sons were trained in the 'Roman law' practised on the continent and still the basis of modern Scottish law, or in medicine or – with an eye on the upper echelons – the priesthood. They taught at the universities, of which there were three by 1495. The heads of these families had no private armies and were dependent on the king, as he was on them. With the wealthier merchant-burgesses, they formed the backbone of the nation. From them would come the reformers, the thinkers and scientists of centuries yet to come. Despite the small numbers of this group, they were a highly significant part of the community.

The tasks of government were increasing. As a trading nation, Scotland was engaged across all of northern Europe. For the political nation, diplomacy was becoming more demanding. The country had acquired a number of armed ships which could be put into action either in the defence of the realm or in the pursuit of piracy (Scots had a deservedly bad name for piracy right across the North Sea). In the time of James IV, the fleet was enlarged, with 'royal ships' including the famous *Great Michael* built specifically for warfare. A Scottish squadron was sent in 1502 to assist the Danes against a Swedish revolt in the Baltic. Towards the end of the fifteenth century, there was a general recession in trade throughout Europe, and Scotland suffered from this. Economic management was not yet a skill expected of government. With one of the most notoriously debased coinages in Europe, Scottish traders had a difficult time, and had to buy harder currencies to finance their business.

Possession of powerful ships helped James IV to make some progress in the long business of bringing the Highlands fully under governmental control. In 1493, the titles and lands of the Lords of the Isles were annexed to the crown. Between then and 1498, the king made several expeditions to try to enforce the reality of his rule on chiefs who promised submission only to

abandon it as soon as the royal force had sailed away
– on one occasion hanging the captain of the royal
garrison at Dunaverty Castle in Kintyre while the royal
ships were still in sight. In 1500, the Earl of Argyll was
made Lieutenant-General for Argyll and the Isles, and a
similar commission was given to the Earl of Huntly two
years later, the hereditary Sheriffdom of Inverness, with
a mandate to enforce peace in the north. As the king's
agents, they had sweeping powers, which they inevitably
exercised for the benefit of the Campbell and Gordon
families respectively. Many small clans were dispossessed
or absorbed into the growing empires of the two earls.
But the culture of feud and raid was not broken, and
the Highlands remained only partly integrated into the
kingdom of Scotland.

James IV's marriage to Margaret Tudor, sister of
Henry VIII, had been marked by a Treaty of Perpetual
Peace with England, which did not long survive the
accession of his brother-in-law as English king. One
issue in Henry's long struggle to father an heir was that
his sister, Margaret, Queen of Scotland, was his heir
presumptive. In 1509, she produced a son. The prospect
of a Stewart king of England was one to bedazzle James
IV.

In 1511, despite the treaty with England, a new treaty of
alliance was made with France, whose king had promised
backing not only for James's proposed crusade to the
Holy Land, but also for any justifiable claim that could
be made for the throne of England. As England, allied
with the Holy League of Pope Julius II, moved towards

war with France, Scottish diplomacy made futile efforts to reconcile the French and the papacy. In 1513, as Henry VIII invaded France, James IV mobilised his fleet and summoned his land forces for an invasion of England. On 9 September, just over the border at Flodden, his army met a hastily recruited English force led by the Earl of Surrey. With around 20,000 men on each side, it was a long and bloody struggle, ending in the complete defeat of the Scots, the death of their king and a number of his lords, and some 10,000 of his countrymen. The English losses also were great, too great for them to follow up the victory, though part of the defensive wall put up by the terror-struck citizens of Edinburgh, in the hope of holding them off, can still be seen today.

CHAPTER SIX

A Nation Reformed,
1513–1603

James IV was keen to present himself as a player in the wider forum of European monarchy. He corresponded widely, promoted his crusade, and made vigorous attempts to exert leverage in the relations between England and France. Scotland had a Spanish ambassador at a time when Spain was keen to end hostility between Scotland and England, the observant Don Pedro de Ayala, whose reports still make lively reading. Scotland's English policy, at first hostile, veered to friendliness, confirmed by James's marriage to King Henry VII's daughter, Margaret, in 1503, which was hymned by the court poet, William Dunbar, as 'the marriage of the Thistle and the Rose'. After the shock of Flodden, the focus of Scottish diplomacy narrowed to France and England. Neither of these nations had any interest in the survival of Scotland as a truly independent state; they did not want to have to continually bargain with the Scots, but to secure them permanently within the French, or English, embrace.

A French Regency

Within Scotland, at least among those in a position to be interested or involved, there was an English party and a French party. The former was headed by the queen, who within a year married Archibald Douglas, Earl of Angus. As James V was less than two years old, the regency was given to his uncle, John Stewart, Duke of Albany, whose sympathies were pro-French.

By 1517, Albany, tired of the endless pattern of arguments, brawls, sieges, submissions and re-offences by the Douglases and their supporters, retired to France, leaving a council of regency to run things. The irreconcilable views of its leading members, the Earl of Angus and the pro-French Earl of Arran, made this impossible, and in 1520 their factions battled it out in the streets of Edinburgh. Angus was effectively in power until Albany came back from France in 1521. The duke's return had more to do with French affairs than Scottish ones. France and England were at war and Scotland was again being required to provide a diversion in the north. But memories of 1513 were too fresh, and the interest of the English party too strong, for Albany to do anything more than strike a gesture. He returned to France in 1524; his departure leaving Angus as master of the king's person and of the kingdom.

Faithful to the practice of the Scottish nobility, the earl ruled not for his young sovereign but for himself, his family, and his large retinue of friends and dependents. To paraphrase the sixteenth-century chronicler, Robert Lindsay of Pitscottie, Angus used the king's authority and the king's law to plunder the country as he pleased. In the process, Angus made a wide range of enemies, and when the king finally escaped his 'protection' in

1528, it took James only two days to raise a force large enough to send Angus to England in a hurry.

The Reign of James V

Once again, the process of reconstituting a royal government began. As ever, the extremities of the kingdom had slipped furthest from any kind of attachment to the centre. James V was compelled to give attention to matters in the Borders. The hills and dales on each side of the border between Scotland and England had long been home to tribally organised communities of farmer-fighters whose raids conformed to a sort of rough-and-ready code of 'Border law' and who were supervised, and sometimes encouraged, by royally appointed wardens on both sides. It suited both governments to have these militant encampments, but only when a state of tension(admittedly normal) between the two countries existed. In times of peace, the border reivers were a plague and an embarrassment. Since feuding, robbery, burning, ambush and murder were a way of life, it was hard for them to stop just because the government wanted them to. It was a life that encouraged arrogance and swagger. 'What wants yon rogue that a king should have?' James V is said to have remarked in 1530 at Carlanrigg in Teviotdale as he met with the finely-attired Johnnie Armstrong of Gilnockie. Johnnie and his retainers were summarily hanged on the surrounding trees.

As with the Highlands, a swift in-and-out punitive visit, though it might dispose of a few leaders, could do nothing to eradicate a long-standing tradition of violence and semi-independence, and left a spirit of resentment and disaffection. The border reivers would maintain their way of life for another 70 years. In the Highlands, though Campbells and Gordons maintained their royal lieutenancies, clan feuds and wars went on as before. In 1540, the king made a voyage round the north and west coasts, accepting the homage of lords and chiefs, and taking numerous hostages as guarantees of future good behaviour.

External policy tilted towards the French interest, underlined by the king's two successive marriages to well-dowered French brides. Henry VIII of England was an uncomfortable neighbour, anxious, as his break with the papacy became complete, to encourage a similar reaction in Scotland. By 1539, the abbeys and priories of England had been abolished. But under James V's government, Scotland remained part of Catholic Europe, though the church paid heavily for its continuing role. The bishops and abbots were compelled to agree to a new tax, which was in theory intended to support the new College of Justice, a much-needed reform of application of the laws of the land. This was the inception of the Court of Session, which was further developed in the 1550s to become both a high court and a court of appeal.

The Decay of the Church

Despite the religious orthodoxy of the government and the resultant burning of heretics, the church was in a decayed state. James V was even more blatant than his predecessors in installing youthful royal offspring in high church positions, and the upper echelons of the nobility were equally greedy in seizing control of rich abbeys.

Sir David Lindsay's verse drama *Ane Satyre of the Thrie Estaitis* ('A Satire of the Three Estates'), first performed in 1540 in Linlithgow Palace, contains some powerful criticisms of political and ecclesiastical life at the time. One of the characters, the Pardoner, expresses the cheerful wish that some prominent Reformers had been smothered in their cradles:

> Als I pray to the Rude
> That Martin Luther, that fals loun,
> Black Bullinger, and Melancthoun,
> Had been smorde in their cude!

But the Pardoner himself is portrayed as a far from reputable figure, offering the remission of sins to anyone who will buy from him such dubious relics as Finn MacCumhal's (MacCool) right shoulder blade, or the rope that hanged Johnnie Armstrong (he who has this, says the crafty Pardoner, will never fear drowning). Lindsay's work, written for court circles and subsequently popularised for less noble audiences, includes 'The Complaynt of the Common Weill of Scotland' and 'The Dreme of the Realm of Scotland'. These poems lamenting the state of the nation were among the most influential texts ever written in Scotland: they were much reprinted, learned by rote, cherished and preserved for three centuries by the common people, and did a great deal to inculcate a national sense of scepticism about those in authority. 'John of the Common Weill' finds that neither in the Borders, Highlands or Lowlands is there the possibility of leading an honest, peaceful, productive life. In the 'Dream', Lindsay concludes:

> Justice may nocht have dominatioun
> But where Peace makes habitatioun.

But in the Scotland of his day, Lindsay found little of either and he asked, rhetorically, why a land of such potential, with a people of such gifts, should remain so poverty-stricken. The answer was plain enough: the life-blood of the country was being sucked out by the rivalry, warfare and greed of the nobility. In central Europe, the reformist doctrines of Lindsay's 'fals loun', Luther, had spread fast. By 1532, Calvin was preaching his version of reform in Paris. Scotland could not remain ignorant of, or immune to, those developments. The church was in no position to defend its doctrine or the way in which it provided spiritual rule. Among the ranks of ordinary priests there was unrest and resentment, and many, including John Knox, adopted Protestantism.

The Decline of James V

In 1533, Henry VIII had been excommunicated by the Pope and had made himself head of the Church of England. His threatening posture became more pronounced, and James V's responses were shifty and weak. Despite a further Treaty of Perpetual Peace made in 1534, by 1542 there were open hostilities between both countries, by land and sea. James had fallen ill and relinquished any attempt to control affairs. In November 1542, on his deathbed, he heard the news of an English victory against a large but poorly led Scottish army at Solway Moss. He had only one living child, a week-old daughter, Mary.

The 'Rough Wooing'

Once again, there was a pro-French and a pro-English party. This time, however, the choice was complicated by the religious divide. The French party was identified with Catholicism, the English one with the now strongly emergent Protestant form of religion. This new dimension brought the range of choice and responsibility right down to the most humble citizens. Their loyalty was demanded by the church. But the new religious ideas, hatched in Saxony and, above all, in Geneva, where Calvin had established a state ruled by religion, were being strongly preached by missionaries every bit as militant and committed as the men who had brought Christianity to the country a thousand years before. These ideas had a strong appeal. Basic to them was the notion that each man and woman had a direct relationship with God. It was a stark, austere creed that people responded to readily.

Led by the queen-mother, Mary of Guise, and Cardinal David Beaton, both head of the church and chancellor of the kingdom, the French party was a strong one, with tradition also on its side. But the initiative was taken by pro-English elements, who imprisoned the cardinal. In 1543, Henry VIII arranged the Treaty of Greenwich, similar to the thirteenth-century Treaty of Birgham, providing for his heir, Prince Edward, to marry the infant Mary. The regency government led by the Earl of Arran then veered away from England to France, with Beaton, released from captivity, strongly urging this policy. The English king began his 'rough wooing' on behalf of his son, making armed incursions by land and sea, and exerting heavy influence on his own paid clients in the Protestant camp. In 1546, a party of Protestant activists broke into St Andrews Castle and assassinated Cardinal Beaton. The aggressive English policy continued after Henry's death, and the heavy Scottish defeat at the battle of Pinkie, outside Edinburgh, in 1548, prompted the decision to appeal for French help, and to send the young queen to France, both for her education and protection.

Mary is Sent to France

On 7 August 1548, a French vessel left Dumbarton with the queen, her retinue of 'four Maries' (Mary Fleming, Mary Beaton, Mary Livingston and Mary Seton) and an escort of Scots lords and ladies. The Earl of Arran remained titular regent until 1554, when Mary of Guise assumed the role (Arran was awarded the French dukedom of Chatelherault). French and Italian mercenary troops backed up the regime. But among the Scottish nobility, led by Lord James Stewart, an illegitimate son of James V, a strong Protestant party was forming.

In 1558, Mary Queen of Scots was married to the

Dauphin Francis, heir to the French throne. On the death of Mary I of England, the French government openly asserted Mary of Scotland's claim to the crown of England, as great-great grand-daughter of Henry VII, over that of Elizabeth I, whose legitimacy in Catholic eyes was contestable. By a secret agreement, the kingdom of Scotland was ceded to the crown of France if Mary should die without children. In 1559, her husband Francis succeeded to the French crown.

Mary's claim to the kingdom of England was to bedevil and finally wreck her career. The government and ruling families of England had no intention of allowing a Catholic claimant, backed by France, to assume the English throne. In the summer of 1560, her mother, Mary of Guise, the regent of Scotland, died and at the end of that year her young husband also died. She was just nineteen, a dowager queen of France, but at an age when she could assume active rule of the country she had left at the age of six.

Mary Returns to Scotland

When Mary landed at Leith in August 1561, Scotland was no longer a Catholic country. 'All revolutions,' said the Scots-Canadian economic historian, J.K. Galbraith, 'consist of the kicking in of a rotten door.' The Protestant revolutionaries, with John Knox as their chief propagandist, had been fighting a war of ideas. Mary of Guise was guardian of the rotten door and she put up a formidable struggle. The war of ideas was won, but it still required the presence of an English fleet and army to install a new Protestant regime, acknowledged by the tripartite Scottish-English-French Treaty of Leith in 1560.

Scotland's first Protestant parliament sat in August 1560 and abolished all authority of the Pope and the celebration of the mass. The Protestant Confession of Faith was to be the basis of religious life. French influence was ended. But the relationship with England was a profoundly uneasy one, warped by the different forms of Protestantism in each country and by Mary's wish, if she relinquished her claim to the English throne, to be named as Elizabeth's presumptive heir. Within Scotland there was another uneasy state of compromise between a Catholic queen and a Protestant parliament. Moderate Protestants like Mary's adviser, William Maitland of Lethington, and James Stewart, made Earl of Moray by his half-sister, advised her to accept the new *status quo*.

There was no real choice. There was still a large Catholic element among the people and among the nobility, but no leading figure. Mary's government was forced to mount an armed campaign against the greatest Catholic magnate, the Earl of Huntly, for rebellion, but his motives were personal ones of the old-fashioned kind.

Meanwhile the reformers were also finding that the realities of power could bring disappointment. The great revenues of the church, which they had hoped to divert to religion and education in the new scheme of things, were also eyed by the government and the nobles, who were in a stronger position to take control of them. The new kirk eventually received a third, or less, of what it had hoped to dispose of.

But below the surface events of Mary's reign, the Scottish reformation was gradually and steadily consolidated and the Church of Scotland, a congregation of ministers and people, with no appointed hierarchy and an elected leadership, became established. By 1578, under the leadership of Andrew Melville, its organisation was completed, with all the steps of administration from the parish kirk session through district presbyteries to the general assembly.

The Collapse of Mary's Rule

The queen's real troubles began with her disastrous marriage to her cousin, Henry Stewart, Lord Darnley, in 1565. 'King' Henry was a worthless and vicious figure who soon became distanced from the queen, and who was assassinated, almost certainly on the orders of the Earl of Bothwell, in February 1567. Bothwell may have seemed the strong man the queen had sought in vain to find in Darnley, but her marriage to him immediately after Darnley's death brought about a major revolt of other Protestant lords, abetted by the kirk. For a time, Mary was a prisoner, forced to abdicate in favour of her and Darnley's infant son James. Despite a romantic escape from imprisonment in Loch Leven Castle, and a final battle at Langside, her reign was effectively over when she signed, under duress, the abdication. In 1568, after the defeat at Langside, Mary fled to England, imprisonment and eventual execution.

Queen's Men and King's Men

A time of bitter civil war ensued, in which the dividing lines cut across religious affiliation. Some staunch Protestants, including Kirkcaldy of Grange, one of Cardinal Beaton's killers, were 'Queen's Men' who believed Mary should be reinstated. Moray, as regent, was assassinated by a member of the Hamilton faction. From 1572, the Earl of Morton governed as regent, with English support.

Mary's son, James VI, was brought up under the auspices of the kirk with the intention of providing the state with a model Protestant sovereign under God. The kirk's failure was James's victory. Whether taught by subversive tutors other than the official ones, or by following his own considerable intelligence, he realised that there was no room for an all-powerful church and a ruling king, and acted accordingly. The struggle between the two would set the tone of Stewart rule in Scotland for the next century.

King James VI's Policies

From an early age, James VI clung firmly to the view that it was not for the king to back down. The earnest and repeated attempts of various factions and noble families to seize and control his person taught him a painful but valuable set of lessons about relative power and his own status. James's other key policy was to do nothing – absolutely nothing – that might upset the chance of his also becoming King of England. England might chop off his mother's head; England's government might spread spies throughout his realm – but James was not going to make trouble. He was the presumptive heir to Elizabeth I, who, as time went on, remained unmarried and childless. This was a chance dynastic opportunity that had been latent (off and on) since the marriage of James IV and Margaret Tudor – a potential great leap in the world for the royal Stewarts, but a step into the unknown for their original kingdom.

The 'Black Acts' of 1584 reveal James's first efforts to take control of the church, on the model of the English sovereign. In July 1585, a Treaty of Alliance with England was concluded, and James became a pensioner of Elizabeth, receiving a somewhat erratically paid 5,000 pounds a year. 'No bishop – no king' was one of the catchwords of his reign; the appointment of bishops was a way of imposing a royally controlled structure on the kirk, and he succeeded in installing bishops but failed to equip them with power.

He had other problems, including the Catholic earls with whom, in the person of Huntly, he flirted, but he found them too unpredictable and dangerous. In a furious battle in Glenlivet, in 1594, Huntly defeated a royal army under the Earl of Argyll. Two years before, in the 'Golden Act' – the terminology is Presbyterian – the government had been compelled to accept the supremacy of presbyteries in the kirk; by 1596 the Black Acts were back and the king was firmly in control.

His management of affairs extended to finance and law: eight Commissioners of the Exchequer were appointed, functionaries whose job it was to see that the king's income – still synonymous with that of the government – was fully paid up; and the Court of Session was put on a more systematic basis, with the appointment of eight senior judges. Efforts were also made to find reliable and respectable men in towns and country areas who would act as impartial king's commissioners and justices to deal with minor offences – this was only accomplished to a limited extent. The laws of the country, though based on the same 'Roman code' as those of France and other European states, remained full of anomalies and archaic provisions. In all parts of the country, any man of position accused of misdemeanour would appear at his trial with an intimidating 'tail' of armed men. Feuds and private battles still went on.

In parliament, the clerical element was now supplied by the reformed kirk. Ever since the time of James I, the king and his close advisers had employed a means of ensuring parliament's acts reflected their wishes. This was through the Committee of the Articles, a small body drawn from all three estates, which drew up the enactments, which the complete parliament then only had to ratify. Successive kings found it convenient and desirable to ensure that the 'Lords of the Articles' were safe men.

The other main instrument of government was the long-established king's council. Convened by the chancellor, it included the hereditary officers of state, and a selection of hereditary nobles chosen either for their power or for their loyalty. Under James VI this body was about 30 strong. Its decisions had the force of acts of parliament, though parliament was usually required to ratify them. The council was a tool of autocratic or aristocratic rule, but when kirk or burgh matters were involved, two non-voting members from each of these 'estates' were co-opted.

The summoning of a parliament was a cumbersome and lengthy business, and for occasions when it was necessary to demonstrate an authority more national than that of the council, the Convention of the Estates was devised. This was an *ad hoc* gathering of picked representatives from the nobility, the officers of state, the church and the burghs. Thirty-seven of them convened to make the 1585 treaty with England, of whom thirteen were burgesses and ten clerics.

Development of the 'organs' of government and the continuing rise of the administrative and legal cadre were to be very important to James VI. In March 1603, on the death of Elizabeth I of England, the long-awaited and much-prepared-for moment at last came when, as her nearest heir, he inherited the crown of England. There was no question of ruling the two countries from the capital of Scotland. James set off for London with the minimum of delay.

CHAPTER SEVEN

Covenants and Coal Mines, 1603–1707

Constitutionally there was a new situation. James VI was king of two separate and independent kingdoms. His ambition was to unite them as a single realm but opposition in England prevented that from happening. Scotland, with its internal disorders, its notorious wild Highlanders, its debased currency, had generally lower living standards than England. Poverty was general and beggary was rife. The squires of England wanted no influx of 'beggarly Scots', and the merchants of England would not contemplate allowing their Scottish competitors free access to their markets. Two nations lived under one crown, but the progress of Scottish trade and industry was hampered by English obstruction.

Another important difference separated the two countries. Throughout the seventeenth century, religion and politics were inextricably intertwined. Scotland was one of the very few states in Europe where the Protestant reformation had been accomplished by a popular revolution, rather than by imposition from above. The Church of England had been established by the king, who was its supreme head. The Church of Scotland had been established in the teeth of royal resistance and did not regard itself as answerable to the king. Despite James VI's imposition of an episcopal structure, this remained a fundamental difference, and one that would have a great influence on later events.

Life Without the King

As he himself boasted, James VI ruled Scotland from far off, by the pen, more effectively than his predecessors had with the sword. The council and the Committee of the Articles were his main instruments. The former was effective enough to have the Earl of Orkney, Patrick Stewart, arrested and executed for his repressive rule, banditry and piracy. The Borders were forcibly tamed by government onslaughts from both sides, and many families left to settle in Northern Ireland – Ireland was also now part of James's domains. In the Highlands, which still held between a third and a half of the population, and where Gaelic remained the language of the people, the power of the Campbells in the west and the Gordons in the east had continued to grow. The clan system prevailed, and the rivalries and hostilities between clans were served and increased by the 'sorners', unproductive fighting men who were maintained by the chief as his army and 'tail'.

The Presbyterian church was slow to make inroads in the Highlands and Islands. The crown's intentional use of bishops as part of the structure of rule was shown by the active work of Andrew Knox, Bishop of the Isles, who induced a number of Hebridean chiefs to sign the Statutes of Icolmkill (Iona) in 1609, which committed them to send their sons out of the Highlands for education. The statutes were also aimed against the

Gaelic bards maintained by the chiefs, and the excessive consumption of wine. Their impact was small, but a sign of the steady, unrelenting and ultimately successful pressure that would continue towards the destruction of the Highland culture and way of life. James VI regarded the Highlanders, and even more so the Islanders, as barbarians. His council in 1597 attempted to settle the Isle of Lewis with new inhabitants from Fife, but the experimental 'plantation' was a disastrous failure, from which the 'Fife Adventurers' returned within two years, leaving the island to its Gaelic-speaking inhabitants.

On his one return to Scotland, in 1617, the king attempted to establish the 'Five Articles', which were designed to bring Scottish church practice more into line with that of the Church of England. Fiercely denounced by the Presbyterian clergy, they were passed by the general assembly of 1618, but were largely ignored in actual practice.

James's Successor – Charles I

When James's son, Charles I, ascended the throne in 1625, he took his responsibilities as head of the church extremely seriously. His first impact on Scottish life resulted from the Act of Revocation of 1625, which was intended to secure for the crown all property that had belonged to the church in 1540. As almost all this land was now in the possession of Scots noble families, his action was deeply resented, and was watered down in subsequent legislation. Charles's policies for reform of church practice were more vigorously enforced. A new *Revised Prayer Book* was introduced to the Scottish Church in 1637 and provoked a riot in St Giles' Church in Edinburgh, which had been promoted to a cathedral under Charles's new dispositions.

More formidably, a group of lords, ministers and burgesses organised an official resistance party against the royal attempts to anglicanise the kirk. They were known as 'The Tables' because in their discussions with the council they sat at separate tables in Parliament House. The king's response was to deem it treason, but there was no royal army in Scotland to put down protest. The Tables drew up a celebrated document, the National Covenant, which pledged its signatories to defend 'the true religion and his Majesty's authority', but there was no doubt about which came first. Many thousands of people signed the National Covenant from the day of its display in Greyfriars' Churchyard in Edinburgh, on 28 February 1638, and Presbyterian fervour reached a height not known since 1560. In November 1638, a general assembly, convened in the king's name, refused to be closed down in his name, and sat on to abolish bishops, condemn the Five Articles and ban Charles's prayer book. Treason had moved on to rebellion, though no war was declared.

A Covenanting Army

In the spring of 1639, an army was mustered and marched south into England. Its intention was to make clear to Charles I that the Scots were willing to fight; its hope was that he would back down. Its confidence was increased by the fact that Charles I could not raise a royal army without summoning a parliament in London; something he could not do without making concessions unacceptable to himself. He had allies in Scotland, the Marquis of Huntly and the Marquis of Hamilton, but the Earl of Montrose captured Aberdeen and took Huntly prisoner.

The affair ended in the Pacification of Berwick, in June 1639, though this was seen by both sides as a delaying tactic before the struggle was renewed.

The abolition of bishops was confirmed by the parliament of 1640. By August of that year, Charles I had succeeded in putting together an army to support his battered authority. The Scots army, led by veterans of European warfare, was mustered again, won an easy victory, and occupied Newcastle and Durham. Although retracing ground familiar to their ancestors, this was in no sense an anti-English war; and in fact the Covenant leaders and the English Parliamentary party were in alliance.

Aware of impending crisis with the parliament in England, Charles made a visit to Edinburgh in 1641, hoping to find allies but only having to make further concessions to the now all-powerful Covenanting leaders, headed by the Marquis of Argyll.

Civil War in England

In August 1642, the civil war in England began, with Scotland officially adopting a neutral position. Argyll's party was in favour of providing active help to the

English parliament, but the Marquis of Hamilton, head of the council, led another group that favoured the king so long as he would guarantee Presbyterianism in Scotland. In the end, the pro-parliament faction prevailed, and in September 1643 the Solemn League and Covenant was agreed between the Scottish and English parliaments. This bound the signatories to: 'bring the Churches of God in the three Kingdoms to the nearest conjunction and uniformity in religion, according to the Word of God and the example of the best reformed Churches.' In the eyes of the Scots, no one needed to look further than their own homeland for the best example.

A large Scottish army led by David Leslie, Earl of Leven, joined the English Parliamentary forces and helped win the battle of Marston Moor in July 1644. But the king found a surprise ally in the Earl of Montrose, who judged that Charles had granted all that the Covenanters had wanted and should therefore be supported. The embattled king made him the royal lieutenant in the Highlands and, at the head of a small but tough and mobile army, mostly of Ulstermen and Islesmen, he conducted a brilliant campaign through the north-east and the Highlands in 1644–45, severely embarrassing the Covenanting leaders and Argyll in particular. By 17 August 1645, he had taken Edinburgh, except for the castle. But on 12 September of that year, his depleted army was defeated by David Leslie at Philiphaugh, near Selkirk. Montrose escaped, first to the north, then in 1646 to France. Covenanter rule was restored.

Charles I Surrenders

On 5 May 1646, Charles I surrendered himself to the Scottish army at Newark on Trent. But the Scots leadership would not back him unless he subscribed to the Covenant, and this he would not do. On 30 January 1647, the Scots handed the king over to the English Parliamentarians, accepted half of the 400,000 pounds they were owed as back pay, and returned across the border.

In a last diplomatic throw, the king made what was known as the 'Engagement' between himself and a group of Scottish nobles, by which he would confirm the Covenant in Scotland, and try an experimental Presbyterianism in England. Breaking from the Covenanting party, the Engagers' army, led by Hamilton, now a duke, went south on the king's behalf. They were defeated by Oliver Cromwell at Preston in July 1648. Retribution followed on all who had supported the Engagement in Scotland. For a time, the most ardent of the Presbyterians, the Whiggamores or Whigs, established a total religious tyranny.

Charles II is Crowned King of Scots

After the execution of Charles I on 30 January 1649, his son, in exile, was immediately proclaimed king in Edinburgh, though he was to have no authority until he had signed up to the Solemn League and Covenant. But Charles II was wary about acceding to the Covenant and in 1650 he sent Montrose to Scotland to promote a royalist rising without Covenanter support. The venture was a failure. Montrose was captured in Sutherland, and tried and hanged in Edinburgh in May, cynically disowned by his royal master. Charles II then signed both the National Covenant and the Solemn League and Covenant. At Scone on 1 January 1651, he was crowned King of Scots.

But the regicide English government, victorious at home, now turned its attention on Scotland. Oliver Cromwell defeated the Covenanter army at Dunbar; and when Charles II invaded England with a large Scottish army, Cromwell defeated it at Worcester in September 1651. Charles II fled abroad. Scotland, its change of fortune from the confident dominance of 1639 complete, was forced into a form of union with England. Thirty Scots members served in Lord Protector Cromwell's London parliament.

A Protectorate Government

Defeat brought peace to a country whose agriculture and economy had been badly hit by warfare and social disruption. For the first time, a standing army – paid for by taxes – based at garrisons throughout the country, ensured peace. For the first time also, the Scottish nobility played no part in the government of the country; indeed Cromwell proclaimed that he had freed Scots 'of the meaner sort' from their lords. Under General Monk, Cromwell's lieutenant, administration was more rigorous and efficient than had been usual in the past. Defeat did not humble the more extreme Presbyterians, who put the failure down to their compatriots' lack of faith, but they were unable to overturn the Protectorate government's tolerance of other sects.

The Restoration Parliament

The interlude of enforced calm ended with the collapse of the Protectorate in 1660 and the return of Charles II to London. A new Restoration parliament, also known as the 'Drunken Parliament', sat in Edinburgh in January 1661. An all-embracing Act Rescissory annulled every act passed after 1633. It was instantly clear that Charles II did not see himself as a 'Covenanted King'. Bishops were reintroduced to the kirk. By the end of 1661, there was an Archbishop of St Andrews, James Sharp, a one-time Presbyterian minister. In 1662, the Covenant was declared illegal. The right of congregations to choose their ministers was removed – this patronage was given to the laird and the bishop to exercise. All ministers had to have their positions confirmed by laird and bishop, and were given until 13 February 1663 to conform to the new conditions.

This was to turn the screw down hard on the people who had flocked – mostly with great enthusiasm – to sign the National Covenant in 1638. Some 260 ministers walked out rather than conform, most of them from the south-west and from Fife. They were replaced by 'curates' of little training whom the theologically seasoned congregations treated with derision. The faithful worshippers gathered with their 'outed' clergy in open-air gatherings known as conventicles. These were declared illegal by the government but in the eyes of the righteous that simply increased their justification. Mounted troops hunted out the conventicles, and those who attended were fined. Stories of atrocities by the dragoons soon spread. A somewhat motley army of Galloway Whigs marched on Edinburgh in November 1666, but were dispersed by regular troops at Rullion Green; the subsequent executions and transportations helped create martyrs.

For 20 years – half the average lifetime in those days – official insistence and popular intransigence rubbed the country raw. Many people whose views were moderate, or who were not prepared to confront bayonets, were disturbed by the persecution of the Whigs. Archbishop Sharp was waylaid and murdered near St Andrews in May 1679, and in the same month an armed band of Covenanters defeated a government force at Drumclog and went on to occupy Glasgow.

On June 22, at Bothwell Brig, south of Glasgow, they were heavily defeated by a government army. After that, the number of Covenanters still in arms was very small, but highly vocal and influential. Known as the Cameronians after their leader Richard Cameron, 'the Lion of the Covenant', they preached complete civil disobedience and claimed it was acceptable to God to kill those who were seeking to kill them. This was the period known as the 'Killing Time'.

The administration was backed up by a widespread system of informers and spies, and the arrival in Edinburgh in 1679 of the king's brother, James, Duke of Albany and York, as Commissioner for Scotland, was an indication that the government had no plans to back down.

The government of Scotland was headed by a secretary of state, based in London. As an aristocratic government, its economic policy was conservative; but it could take unpopular decisions. In 1672, the Privy Council abolished many of the trade monopolies of the royal burghs, which had been stoutly defended for centuries, leaving them with low-volume, high-value imports only. Markets and fairs could now be licensed outside the royal burghs, and newer towns, such as Greenock and Bo'ness, began to grow. The government was also corrupt. The grandees who controlled trade and taxation, whether nationally or locally, made sure that their own fortunes were increased as a result.

First Signs of the Enlightenment and the Industrial Revolution

Writers on Scottish history often remark that the Renaissance had a relatively minor impact on Scotland, and in the field of fine arts this observation has some truth. But the Renaissance was equally important in the fields of science and engineering (Leonardo da Vinci comes to mind) and these were evident in seventeenth-century Scotland, which in spite of the religious dispute, saw developments in these fields, both borrowing from Europe and contributing new ideas. With four universities (Edinburgh University was founded in 1582), the country did not lack intellectual centres, and the spread of knowledge encouraged the more enterprising members of the landed class to look at the resources of their land and exploit or enhance these. Coal and salt became economically important, with much of the coal being used to boil seawater in the salt pans. At Culross, a coal pit was dug whose shafts extended under the sea and which was drained by a water-driven bucket chain. The first signs of the intellectual 'enlightenment' of the eighteenth century, and of the industrial revolution, were very much present in the seventeenth.

It was a time of striking contradictions and uneven trends of development. Along with entrenched Calvinism ran a deep-seated vein of superstition which resulted in belief in witches and the consequent persecution of lonely old women. Logarithms were first worked out in Edinburgh by John Napier (1614), and by the mid-century the country was being mapped to the highest standard of the time. In 1679, the laws were at last organised and codified by James Dalrymple, later Lord Stair, in the *Institutions of the Law of Scotland*. The first book on Scottish horticulture, John Reid's *The Scots Gardiner*, appeared in 1683. The grim keeps of the nobility, at least in the Lowlands, began to acquire new inner buildings with big windows and comfortable interiors, and sometimes were wholly replaced by Palladian mansions. Older ways were maintained in many rural districts, and most country people still lived in the primitive style of their ancestors, in low, sooty houses with a central hearth.

Farmers, Cattle Drovers and Traders

The Border country, tamed early in the seventeenth century, was becoming a region of farmland, and sheep grazed in the dales where the border reivers had once gone riding out on foray. Nor were the Highlands, a much greater and more rugged extent of country, immune to change. The small black cattle, bred in the hills, became an important trade commodity during the century, and the economy of the Highlands south of the Great Glen was boosted by the cattle trade. Most of the profit went to the men who controlled great estates, like the Dukes of Argyll and Montrose, but cattle rearing helped to maintain thousands of families in remote glens. Gaelic-speaking, still imbued with the old Gaelic culture, and still living within the social organisation of the clan, they were as foreign to their Scots-speaking fellow-countrymen as an Inuit community might have been. And yet there were many links.

Rob Roy MacGregor, cattle drover and trader, and also Jacobite fighter – later to be declared an outlaw – was cousin to James Gregory, professor of medicine at King's College, Aberdeen. This was typical; those who emerged from the Gaelic fastness could be very speedily absorbed into a self-consciously modernising Scotland. The chiefs of all the greater clans, usually earls or lords in their own right, were also links, of a kind. Tradition and the social structure still required them to be Gaelic chiefs among their own people, in something resembling the old patriarchal style. However, they also had lives outside the Highlands, in Edinburgh and even

London, in which their Celtic connections gave them a touch of glamour, but in which they were normally at pains to conform to the conventional view of what a lord should be.

A New Regime

Old attitudes and habits hardened on the accession of James VII in 1685. He was already known to Scotland as the unyielding commissioner, and a practising Catholic. The government in Scotland was headed by the Earl of Perth with his brother, Lord Melfort. Religious toleration was introduced, though conventicles remained illegal, but this was merely seen as part of a programme towards the re-imposition of Catholicism, in a country which for more than a hundred years had been taught to equate the Pope with the Antichrist. It was events in England that brought about the flight of James VII to France and the installation of William of Orange and his wife, Mary Stewart, as joint sovereigns of England in November 1688, but in March 1689 a Convention of the Estates confirmed their rule over Scotland as well. There was a condition attached – episcopacy must be expunged from the Church of Scotland.

By no means everyone supported the new regime. More than 200 ministers refused to renounce the oath they had taken to James VII and were turned out of their churches. Despite the government policy of religious tolerance, Catholics and Episcopalians inclined towards the exiled James VII and, as when Mary I was deposed, there were many who felt that the legitimate king should be supported. Thus the Jacobite movement began. Its early appearance was formidable.

Emergence of the Jacobites

Viscount Dundee, former scourge of the Cameronians, raised a Highland army on behalf of James VII and on 27 July 1689 defeated a government force in the Pass of Killiecrankie. But Dundee was killed in the battle, and without their charismatic general, the Highlanders were defeated at Dunkeld and dispersed. Ironically, the victors of Dunkeld were a Cameronian regiment, no longer victims of persecution but agents of the new order.

Jacobitism remained a powerful force in Scotland, its influence perhaps increased by the fact that the reign of William and Mary coincided with a time of bad harvests and hardship in the country, compounded by economic difficulties and one major financial disaster. Whilst none of this would have been different under James VII, his court in France was a focus for disaffection.

An Economy in Decline

Scottish anger was increased by William's lack of interest in and concern for the country. At a time when trade was increasing, he supported the merchants of London and other English exporting ports in closing off markets from Scotland. Tariffs were imposed on the sale of Scottish coal and salt in England. In this era of early capitalism, many countries set up tariff barriers to protect their own industries. Scotland was a trading nation without the freedom to formulate its own foreign policy. Its exports were mostly low-value bulk commodities of mediocre quality, such as coal, wool, and salt – all susceptible to home competition in other markets, and the economy went into sharp decline.

The Massacre of Glencoe

One notorious instance illustrates the attitude and nature of the government of Scotland in the reign of William and Mary. Since 1689 the potential for trouble in the Jacobite Highlands had been obvious, and those in power gave much thought to containing or eliminating the threat. Carrots and sticks were the inevitable tools. The carrot was a large sum of money entrusted to the Campbell Earl of Breadalbane to purchase the loyalty or co-operation of clan chiefs: the money was never satisfactorily accounted for but the supposition remained that little of it had got past the earl. The stick was an oath of allegiance, to be sworn to the new monarchs by all the clan chiefs who had fought against them. This was to be accomplished by 1 January 1692 – failure to do so would result in unspecified penalties. All signed – with James VII's special dispensation in some cases – but the chief of the Macdonalds of Glencoe was five days late. The Glencoe Macdonalds, a small clan not averse to cattle-lifting, had been an irritation to the Earl of Breadalbane. The joint secretary of state, Sir John Dalrymple of Stair, was keen to show that the government could strike hard into the Highlands. He failed to tell the Privy Council of Macdonald's belated signature, and obtained a royal warrant for the annihilation of the Glencoe Macdonalds. A detachment of Campbell troops was sent to Glencoe, ostensibly to be billeted there, and were hospitably received. About a week later, during the night of 13 February 1692, they turned on their hosts, killing some 38 men, women and children, and driving many others out into the snow in search of escape. Clan warfare had seen worse, but this was cold-blooded massacre planned by a government supposedly acting within the rule of law, and it left a permanent stigma on those who planned and carried it out.

The Road to Union
There was further bitterness when the ambitious project for a 'Company of Scotland Trading to Africa and the Indies' was stifled by English opposition. The collapse in 1699 of the ambitious venture to establish a Scottish colony in Darien, on the central American isthmus, not only brought financial loss to all who had invested in it, but delivered a massive psychological blow. The Scottish aspiration to join other European countries in the hunt for colonial territory and wealth had been rudely choked off. The scheme had been absurdly over-optimistic, but once again the 'Revolution' government could be blamed. As a result, relations between Scotland and England sank to a level of hostility that was little short of actual war. But Scotland was not in a condition to wage war.

Observers on both sides of the border could see

that this state of things could not be continued. The alternatives were complete union with England, or a separate kingship of Scotland. William of Orange died in 1702 with matters unresolved, and still deteriorating. His successor, Anne, younger daughter of James VII, convened a gathering of Scottish and English commissioners to consider a Treaty of Union late in 1702, but it collapsed. The English side would not agree to the shared level base of opportunity which alone would make a union work. Three more years of hostile gestures, angry pamphlets, unpaid official salaries, and falling trade ensued before negotiations finally got under way in April 1706. The Scottish negotiators had been picked to be acceptable to the English side. Their strongest card was that their parliament, unlike that of England, had not committed itself to who would follow Anne on the throne (she had outlived her many children). England was committed to the Elector of Hanover. James VII had died in 1701, but his son, also a James, remained available, in theory at least, to the Scots. But the prospect of a stoutly Catholic dynasty being accepted in an overwhelmingly Presbyterian country was deeply improbable, despite its Scottish pedigree.

A draft Treaty of Union was achieved by September 1706. A storm of controversy accompanied it. The opposition included the Presbyterian clergy, the royal burghs, and many of the more enterprising lairds, of whom the most vocal was Andrew Fletcher of Saltoun. Under the management of the Duke of Queensberry, the treaty was fiercely debated and argued over, clause by clause. But, clause by clause, it was passed. The final act came on 16 January 1707, and on 1 May of that year, the United Kingdom of Great Britain became an established political unit.

CHAPTER EIGHT

From Union to Empire,
1707–1800

The union with England was not welcomed by the Scottish people. The Edinburgh city mob had railed at the pro-union members of parliament. Up and down the country, the view was that bribery and the self-interest of a few had won the day. Some supported the union for pragmatic reasons, knowing the perilous state of the national finances and believing that England, growing ever richer with its colonial empire, would always obstruct the aspirations of an independent Scotland, but such a view scarcely generated enthusiasm for the new state of things. The great debate had nevertheless stirred up a Scottish self-awareness which, despite the loss of political independence, remained vigorous.

Scotland After the Treaty of Union

It was not long before doubts and concerns were exacerbated by the behaviour of the new parliament of Great Britain, where Scotland was represented by 45 members compared to England's 200 – a reminder that it was not exactly a union of equals. Although the union protected the church and the legal system of Scotland, the combined parliament tampered with both. In 1712, a Patronage Act was passed, once again restoring to lairds the power of appointing the parish minister. The supreme court of Scotland no longer sat in Edinburgh, but was the House of Lords in London, whose members, other than the 16 Scottish peers, knew little and cared less about Scots law. Again in 1712, an increase in the malt tax, not only infringing one of the provisions of the union but pushing up the price of Scots ale, was only frustrated by furious protest. The English system of customs duties was introduced. The Scottish exchequer had rarely taxed imports, and the 'revenue men' who now took up station around the coasts were a focus for hostility. Smuggling became a major industry lasting right through the eighteenth century, and black-market tea, tobacco, wine and gin were sold widely. The Porteous Riots of 1736 in Edinburgh were sparked off when the city guard opened fire on citizens protesting at the hanging of a smuggler. Problems and disadvantages were plain, while the economic benefits predicted by union supporters were slow to materialise. Despite their new legal rights as British citizens, Scots traders found it hard to get a toehold in markets long dominated by English concerns.

Still the union was a reality, accepted as such by the majority of the population. The business of living had to be continued in the new context. The undercurrents of enterprise, invention and improvement, which typified the seventeenth century just as much as religious strife, were strengthened in the eighteenth century by experience, persistence and success. New methods did not always work, but when they did, they provided rewards on a scale not known before.

The Jacobite Uprising of 1715

The speedy installation of George I, Elector of Hanover, as monarch of the United Kingdom in 1714 outraged the Jacobite sympathisers and disturbed many others. James Stewart, 'the Old Pretender', was regarded by many as the true king. But it was September 1715 before a significant reaction took place, when the Earl of Mar (a leading supporter of the union in 1707) proclaimed James VIII as king and raised an army of Highlanders to support his cause. Mar's indecisive leadership soon deprived him of the initiative. The government forces, assembled under the command of the Duke of Argyll, met the Jacobites at Sheriffmuir, above Dunblane. Though the battle itself was inconclusive, it left Argyll in a stronger strategic position. A separate Jacobite force under Brigadier Mackintosh of Borlum had invaded England but was defeated by government troops at Preston. In January 1716, the Pretender landed at Peterhead, but by then the impetus of revolt was petering out; he left again, with Mar, from Montrose on 4 February.

In 1719, a further attempt to start a Jacobite rising was made by George Keith, the hereditary Earl Marischal, who landed in Kintail, in Wester Ross, with a force of Spanish troops. Few came to join him, and his small army was scattered by a government force at the battle of Glenshiel. Jacobitism was by no means dead, but it was increasingly becoming a distraction. Peace between Britain and France had compelled the Pretender's court to remove to Rome, making communication far more difficult. Whilst James and his son, Charles Edward, both appreciated that the Highlands were by far their prime source of armed supporters, their ambitions were never focused on Scotland alone. They wanted to regain England, Wales and Ireland too. The Jacobite clan chiefs were realistic enough to know that a Highland army, unaided, was not going to achieve that.

Developments in Agriculture

More indicative of the general trend of events in Scotland were such things as the formation, in 1723, of the Society for the Improvement of Knowledge in Agriculture, based in Edinburgh. Most of the prominent legal and professional families were also landowners, and 'improvement' was a buzz-word. The old agrarian landscape began to change with better drainage, scientific fertilising, and such new crops as potatoes and turnips. Outside the Highlands and Islands the old runrig system was long outdated. The improvements had strong social implications, however. The farmer-lairds required more ground and bigger fields for their larger-scale operations. Above all, they wanted fewer tenants. Cottars whose families had tilled the ground for generations were forcibly evicted. In Galloway especially, in the early 1720s, this resulted in great unrest, when 'Levellers' tore down the dry-stone walls and thorny hedges put up to enclose the cottars' old open fields. Armed troops were sent in to disperse them, in a manner reminiscent of the attacks on their grandparents' conventicles.

Other Developments

Other modernising trends were becoming apparent. In 1708, Edinburgh University abandoned the old system of teaching by regents, in which one man, rather like the parish schoolmaster, was expected to be master of many subjects. Specialist teaching began. In Glasgow University, to the horror of traditionalists, Francis Hutcheson began in 1729 to lecture on philosophy in English rather than in Latin.

From 1713, turnpike trusts had begun to be established in the Lowlands, to improve the country's wretched road system, while after 1715, for strategic military purposes, a network of roads was built in the central Highlands, linking the new fortresses of Fort George, Fort Augustus and Fort William with the south.

In the 1730s, pioneered by John Cockburn of Ormiston, new villages began to be built, replacing the random arrangement of old-style cottages in farm-toun or clachan (small village) by an orderly street or square of two-storey stone houses. Like many visionary pioneers, Cockburn went bankrupt, but more than a hundred new villages were built in the eighteenth century. Often they were intended to re-house some of those removed from now-enclosed estates, and some became quite prosperous centres of linen-making, sea-fishing and weaving. Others were miserable rustic slums, devoid of activity.

Throughout the country, many small-scale industries were starting up, using water-power and the new technology of steam. Glasgow, second-largest town after Edinburgh, with a population of around 20,000 in the 1720s, found its western location an advantage in exploiting the possibility of trade with the American colonies. Perhaps because of its long non-royal burgh status (its royal charter came in 1611), its ethos had for a long time been more enterprising and commercial than in the nearby older, more staid royal burghs such as Rutherglen and Renfrew – destined to become its suburbs. In 1667, a deep-water harbour had been built downstream at Port Glasgow, and both trade and manufacture developed rapidly through the eighteenth century.

Whether it was produced by the climate of introspection and self-examination created both by the events preceding the union, and the union itself, or whether it was the flowering of an older, more organic stem rooted in the more distant past, a new energy seemed to be at work in Scotland. The mood was practical and pragmatic. Even Jacobite leaders such as the Earl of Mar could be industrialists; in his case as a coal-owner and founder of the Alloa glass-works.

The universities continued the process of reform that resulted in a wider curriculum with specialist teachers. Medicine, physics, chemistry and philosophy began to flourish, though theology remained the prime subject, and the theological influence remained very strong – strong enough to deny David Hume, the country's greatest philosopher and a self-confessed atheist, a professorial chair at Edinburgh. Scotland was the home of both Hume's extreme scepticism and the influential

'Common Sense' school of philosophy, founded by Thomas Reid, which arose in opposition to it. The practical spirit also led to the founding of new schools, known as 'academies', of which Perth's was the first in 1760. In these, the old classically based syllabus still used in the town grammar schools was replaced by a deliberate emphasis on science and commerce. In 1756, one of the first large-scale factories in the world was established on the River Carron, near Falkirk. The Carron Ironworks were saluted sardonically by Robert Burns:

> We cam' na here to view your warks,
> In hopes to be mair wise,
> But only, lest we gang to hell,
> It may be no surprise.

For displaced landworkers, the new factories were the only source of available work, and a drift from the land to the towns began, which would eventually result in the majority of Scots becoming urban rather than country dwellers. For others there were wider opportunities. Although the ambition of John Knox's generation, to put a school in every parish, was never quite fulfilled, Scotland at this time was educating a higher proportion of its young people – particularly young men – than any country in Europe. An education was a passport to wealth and position, and an escape from the drudgery of farm life, with its dull though healthy diet dominated by oatmeal in a variety of forms. For citizens of the United Kingdom, escape could be out of Scotland altogether. Enough 'lads o' pairts' found their way to London for there to be a reaction, part-satiric, part-xenophobic, against the Scots invasion.

The Jacobite Uprising of 1745

The life of this busy, enquiring, pragmatic people was given a sudden jolt in September 1745 when, like all-too-solid ghosts from the far-off past, an army of tartan-clad Highlanders, armed with broadswords and muskets, appeared out of the north and occupied the city of Edinburgh. A government army sent to stop them was defeated in a single devastating charge at Prestonpans. At the head of the Highland army was Prince Charles Edward Stewart, a handsome 24-year-old who had come on his own initiative to reclaim the United Kingdom for his father, the Old Pretender. To the consternation of the Jacobite clan chiefs, he had landed with no men, few arms, and little money.

The prince found few recruits in Edinburgh and the south. It was with a still almost entirely Highland army that he left Edinburgh in November, on the march to England. By 20 December they were back in Scotland, having got within 120 miles of London before turning back. The almost complete lack of English recruits, combined with the mustering of government armies, had convinced the prince's commanders, if not himself, that the capture of London was impossible. In January 1746, the Jacobite army defeated a government force under General 'Hangman' Hawley, at Falkirk but, with the Highland troops eager to go home for the winter, a hold on the south could not be consolidated, and the prince retreated with his men to Inverness. On 16 April, reduced in numbers and morale, his army was confronted at Culloden Moor by the cannons and drilled musketeers commanded by the Duke of Cumberland. Poor tactics on the Jacobite side did not help in what was an inevitable defeat.

For five months, Prince Charles Edward was a fugitive, and for much longer the Highlands were under the heel of an army of occupation. Jacobitism, having been a minor threat, had abruptly shaken the pedestal of power, and power took its revenge. The Highland dress and bagpipe were outlawed – except when worn and played by government regiments – and a determined effort was mounted to stamp out the old Highland way of life.

By the 1740s it was already becoming anachronistic. Government action to reduce the power of chiefs and lords affected also those in the Lowlands and Borders. The 1748 Act for Abolishing Heritable Jurisdictions removed all landlords' rights to control justice, in return for a one-off financial payment of which the lion's share went to the Duke of Argyll, the hereditary Justiciar of Scotland.

In September 1746, a French ship finally plucked the prince away, with around a hundred of his closest supporters. Jacobitism as a political, religious or military threat was now a thing of the past – instead it gained a shadow-life as a nostalgic fantasy which even now is not quite dead.

Changes in the Highlands

In the Highlands, a new reality, which had been making a slow entry for decades, now became the norm. The economic criteria which governed life elsewhere – and which even then were being analysed for the first time by the Kirkcaldy-born Adam Smith, who would go on to publish *The Wealth of Nations* in 1776 – were also applied to a region where wealth had hitherto been measured in men and cattle. The clan chiefs, now landed proprietors, had acquired the same interest as their lowland peers in cash, rents, bank accounts and (in some cases) 'improvement'. They found the large population of native clanspeople paying low rents, mainly in kind, to tacksmen who then passed on their own modest rents to the chief, an encumbrance that stood in the way of getting a good cash income from their land. The pathetic trust and loyalty given to hereditary owners were increasingly ill-repaid. The people were superfluous, except for those coastal and island proprietors who could employ them in the labour-intensive kelp trade: the harvesting and burning of off-shore seaweed to provide alginates for the growing chemical industry of Glasgow and other industrialising centres. There, people were prevented from leaving; elsewhere, their departure was enforced. Grown men could be usefully recruited into newly formed Highland regiments, or pressed into service for the Royal Navy, with a bounty on each man accruing to the laird. Many families, with an especially high proportion from the tacksman class (who held leases on land that they would sublet), left the Highlands of their own accord to find a new life in the south or overseas. But there also began the process of eviction and forcible expulsion which gathered pace in the early nineteenth century as the 'Highland Clearances'. The Gaelic language was still widely spoken, and many traces of the 'Old Highlands' remained in dress (restored in 1782), custom and tradition – though often verging on parody of the one-time real thing, and increasingly shot through by the cannonade of puritanical Presbyterianism as the Reformation finally caught up with the Gaels.

The 'Scottish Dispersion'

By the 1750s, the whole of Scotland was firmly within the confines of the British union and the wider British empire. It was to defend and extend that empire, in North America, the West Indies, and India, that the new regiments were needed, and by the 1790s also to engage in warfare in Europe. The demands of imperial trade and imperial rule also drew heavily on Scots. For almost 200 years, the great majority of the Scottish people would be content to subsume their Scottish identity within a British one, and the 'Scottish dispersion' saw their fellow-citizens taking Scottish names and traditions to South Carolina, Ontario, New Zealand and many other colonies.

Population Growth and its Effects

In the first scientific modern census, the population of Scotland was estimated in 1755 by the Reverend Alexander Webster to be 1,265,000. At that time the majority of the people still lived in an essentially rural setting of farm-touns, new villages, crofting clachans and small market towns. The first official census in 1801 put the figure at 1,608,000.

Despite the work of the 'Improvers', the challenge of feeding this steadily increasing population was severe. Most rural dwellers in the latter part of the eighteenth century lived on a poorer diet than their ancestors of the sixteenth or fifteenth, with a heavy emphasis on oatmeal, and very little in the way of meat or fish. Cattle-raising was concentrated in large estates and focused on export to England via the great drovers' fairs at places like Muir of Ord, Crieff and Falkirk, and only the well-to-do ate meat at all regularly.

Food riots, caused by shortages and the resultant high prices, occurred from time to time – a reminder that for most people the business of keeping themselves and their families on the right side of starvation remained by far the dominant aspect of their lives. Almost everyone was poor, though a few were very rich; but to fall below poverty into destitution was to expect a miserable and early death from Scotland's apocalyptic scourges: disease, exposure, malnutrition and neglect. Care of the helpless was a duty of the kirk session in each parish; but parishes reserved their small funds for their own people and had nothing to offer to the numerous wandering vagrants. Robert Burns's cantata of *The Jolly Beggars,* published in 1799, two years after his death, paints a defiantly vigorous picture of these drop-outs, fugitives and excommunicants who were a familiar part of the national scene. Visitors to Scotland from more prosperous countries had always been plagued by beggars; as far back as the end of the fifteenth century William Dunbar had written in complaint of those who pestered people in the middle of Edinburgh. In the eighteenth century, there was also the more serious threat of gangs who roamed the country looking for able-bodied young men and women to kidnap and sell as slaves in North America. At the same time, a number of shipping families in Greenock and Glasgow were making a good living out of the trade in slaves from Africa to the West Indies and Virginia.

Intellectual Activity

The most visible aspect of the transformation of Scotland into not only a modern society, but one which in some ways led the world of ideas, was the construction of the 'New Town' of Edinburgh, which got under way in 1767. As a grand exercise in town-planning, it matched what was happening in other European cities and showed that the removal first of king and court, then of parliament, had not sucked the spirit out of the capital city. As the headquarters of the law and the church, Edinburgh retained a national status; and from the mid-to-late eighteenth century, it was a source of intellectual stimulus to the world. Though David Hume's *Treatise of Human Nature* fell, as he put it, 'dead-born from the press' in 1739, his work was of profound and continuing importance to modern philosophy. Political economy and geology both had their origins in Edinburgh, and physics, chemistry and medicine were also much advanced.

Scottish influence on European thought was not confined to the rigours of philosophy. In 1760, an enterprising native of Kingussie, James Macpherson, published what he claimed to be verse translations of ancient Gaelic texts – forming an epic poem entitled *Ossian*. Despite much scepticism, *Ossian* and its successive volumes took cultured Europe by storm, riding on and contributing to the wave of interest in a more innocent, natural, heroic past which would result in the Romantic period of European literature, art and music. It was ironic that this should occur at the very time that the traditions of the Highlands were being most remorselessly attacked. A more genuine process of rediscovery also rekindled interest in the ballad tradition of the fifteenth century and earlier. In 1802, Walter Scott, a 31-year-old lawyer, published his collection *Minstrelsy of the Scottish Border*. Scotland, with its misty mountains, its Ossianic heroes, its archaic music, its tartan kilts, became part of European myth. Scott, in the years to come, was to form a national myth out of the same material. With his long series of verse romances, starting with *The Lay of the Last Minstrel* (1805), and then the 'Waverley' novels, he was by far its prime instigator. But others helped. Here is Lord Byron waxing lyrical to the Caledonian Meeting in London, in May 1814:

> Who hath not glow'd above the
> page where fame

Hath fix'd high Caledon's
    unconquer'd name:
The mountain-land which spurned
    the Roman chain,
And baffled back the fiery-crested
    Dane,
Whose bright claymore and
    hardihood of hand
No foe could tame – no tyrant
    could command?

The relevance of this to a nation of iron-puddlers and coal miners, linen weavers and cotton spinners, crofters and farmers, furnace-men and fish-wives, lawyers and engineers, few of whom had ever seen a claymore, was non-existent. Its reiteration, in various ways, throughout the nineteenth century, had an effect on the Scots' self-image which still lingers on in the twenty-first.

A Land of Song, Music and Dance

In case a picture should emerge, from this century and the preceding one, of a sober-minded, intellectual, rather dour population, it is important to remember that there was also laughter and entertainment. A strong and lively tradition of popular song, story, music and dance survived through this period. Most of it was of no great quality or literary merit: many old songs were greatly improved by the genius of Robert Burns, a dedicated collector of traditional material. Entertainment was provided by wandering balladists and street singers, and to an even greater degree by the inexpensive chapbooks, cheaply printed and sold in large quantities by packmen (pedlars). The chapbooks contained a mixture of wild prophecy, traditional folk tales, uplifting items like 'The Ravishing Dying Words of Christina Ker, Who Died at the Age of Seven', and above all humorous narratives and dialogues. The humour was earthy, direct and bawdy, usually set around fairs and village weddings, events which provided a setting for drink and uninhibited behaviour. Ever since the fifteenth-century poem 'Christis Kirk on the Green', accounts of such gatherings had been highly popular. The tradition went on for centuries, reaching its peak in Burns's 'The Holy Fair' and in the nineteenth-century sexual doggerel of 'The Ball of Kirriemuir'.

A Hundred Years of Change

In the hundred years between 1700 and 1800, Scotland had changed from being an old-style primary producer of bulk goods to a new-style commercial and manufacturing country with an infrastructure of banks and technically oriented colleges – especially in Glasgow – to support the continuing growth of industry and the modernisation of agriculture. Interestingly, the role of the clergy in the process was substantial; ministers were usually also farmers of their 'glebes' (the land attached to their church) and took a keen interest in economics and industry even as the Calvinist fervour of the kirk cooled into 'moderation'. The world's first savings bank was set up by Henry Duncan, minister of

Ruthwell parish, Dumfries-shire, in 1810. The business life of Glasgow survived the collapse of its huge tobacco trade when the American War of Independence broke out in 1775, and cotton spinning on an industrial scale helped to replace it. Spinning in factories, and weaving as a home industry, employed large numbers – in 1795, there were an estimated 39,000 handloom weavers at work. Some people thought that progress could hardly go further, but the pace of industrial growth was about to increase dramatically.

CHAPTER NINE

Industry, Reform
and Bad Drains,
1800–1900

The least modern aspect of the country, at the start of the nineteenth century, was its administration. The 45 members of the Commons and the 16 peers still made their way by slow coach or sailing ship to London. The county and burgh members were elected by a very small number of voters, some 2,000 in total, all of them landowners in the counties or prominent burgesses in the towns. Town councils elected their own successors. The provost was very often a prominent local laird rather than a burgess. Much of the towns' common land was taken over by neighbouring landowners by semi-legal means, often in exchange for un-repaid loans.

Corruption was endemic in the system, stemming right from the top, where for three decades, from the eighteenth into the nineteenth century, 'King' Henry Dundas controlled the political life of the country in the Tory interest by handing out, or withdrawing, government-paid jobs. Public office at almost any level was seen as a way of enriching oneself. The Whigs, as opposition party, complained but when they had been in power, by no coincidence, all the Scottish members of parliament had been Whigs. (The terms Whig and

Tory had taken on new meaning since the seventeenth century and now represented 'respectable' political parties.) Real opposition was found among the radicals who sympathised both with revolutionary France and America, but their numbers were small and their attempts to publish their views were heavily suppressed. In the 1790s, when Britain and France were at war, a series of notorious treason trials saw the conviction and transportation to Australia of a group of leading radicals.

The great majority of the population had no say at all in how their communities and country were managed. But anyone with their wits about them (and this was a relatively well-educated country, with a high level of literacy for the time) could find a copy of *The Rights of Man*, or read some of the many pamphlets in prose and verse published by radical thinkers and activists (Paisley was a particular centre of this activity). The argument for democracy was ready-made and would eventually germinate. In the kirk, a similar process was fermenting. Although the union parliament had introduced patronage as long ago as 1712, it had always rankled with a substantial group who harked back to the 'Revolution Settlement' of 1689 and deplored the 'moderation' of their fellows, which they saw as backsliding from the principles of the Scottish Reformation. Although the political reformers and the kirk reformers did not overlap greatly, both groups were reacting against the efforts of a landowning oligarchy to maintain 'establishment' control of an increasingly diverse and complex society.

Both groups would gradually come closer together to help form the Liberal consensus that dominated Scottish politics in the later nineteenth century, but each had first to experience its own crisis when belief and action could no longer be held apart.

The Effects of the Industrial Revolution

Outside the control of any organisation, the process of industrialisation went on, stimulated by the many advances made in using steam technology. As more powerful machinery was introduced, factories sprang up. The demand for coal increased. Uses for iron and other metals multiplied. Canals and railways were built to convey raw materials in and finished products out. The world's first paddle steamer, the *Charlotte Dundas* (1801), was intended as a canal tug-boat.

The population of the industrial centres rose dramatically. By 1801, Edinburgh's long supremacy as the biggest town was lost to Glasgow, which by then had just over 100,000 inhabitants. It would have ten times that number by 1901.

New working conditions determined the pattern of urban growth. Factory workers did not need space for looms in their homes. Street after street of one-room ('single-end') and two-room houses were speedily built and, maintaining an older tradition of domestic housing in towns, thousands of new tenement blocks went up. Planning permission was not required. The owner of the ground was free to develop it, and the nearer the factory was to the workers' houses, the better. The call of its steam whistle could draw them punctually to work at the start of the day. Ignorance, greed and urgency combined to ensure that the close-packed houses had neither adequate water supplies or sewage facilities. Such buildings, soon coated in soot, became instant slum dwellings.

Work was plentifully available – most of the time. The children of the poor in Scotland had always worked. Eight-year-olds now put in a 12-hour day, six days a week, in mine, mill or factory. If, like the young David Livingstone at Blantyre, they wanted schooling, that had to be after their working day. The constraints on commerce and industry were few. Trade recession resulted in lay-offs and unemployment. New technology, such as J.B. Neilson's hot-blast iron-refining process of 1828, using low-grade but easily accessible banded coal and iron ore, or the refining of paraffin from shale-oil, developed by James Young in the late 1840s, could double the population of areas like Lanarkshire and West Lothian with the resultant demand for labour. Diseases like cholera and typhus began to haunt the close-packed, insanitary streets, but despite their culling effect, and a very high rate of infant mortality, the population kept on growing.

The industrial population of Scotland became a proletariat – a term adapted by political economists to denote wage earners who have no savings or financial reserves. Karl Marx saw this class, by far the largest group in a newly industrialised society, as the one which would arise violently, overthrow the forces of capitalism, and institute a utopian state in which the apparatus of government and human management would wither away.

The closest the Scottish workers came to revolt was in the so-called 'Radical War' of 1820. Since the end of the Napoleonic Wars in 1815, there had been an economic slump. Unemployment was high, wages were cut, and the Corn Laws pushed up the price of food. There was great hardship. The old methods of poor relief could not stand up to the demands of densely populated new urban areas. In 1817, a number of radical agitators were put on trial. Newspapers were taxed heavily to deter the poor from buying radical sheets. In 1820, a band of protesters, mostly weavers, demonstrated against employers' refusals to allow a trades union, and against high food prices. Another enemy was the technical progress that was making the weavers' handlooms redundant.

At Bonnymuir, outside Falkirk, there was an encounter with a military force raised by the alarmed authorities. Three men were subsequently hanged, and 19 transported. The government reaction was to crack down harder on dissent. There was no general insurrection in favour of the Bonnymuir marchers. Though protest did not go away, it never went beyond a local, or single-industry, level and the authorities continued to bear down hard. In 1836, cotton workers went on strike for three months, and five leaders were arrested and sentenced to transportation. (They received pardons in 1840 – an indication that justice was lagging some way behind the knee-jerk reaction of the outraged employers.)

New Goals

The Chartist movement, which had begun in England, also had branches and adherents in Scotland. Formed in the wake of the limited parliamentary reforms of 1832, their aims included the abolition of the property qualification for voters, and the institution of a secret ballot in elections. By 1839, the *Scottish Chartist Circular* had 20,000 subscribers and many more readers. The authorities and the owners of land and business viewed them as potential destroyers of society. Though Chartism gradually faded away, a radical strain in the thinking of working people remained.

Nineteenth-century people with a concern for social progress and social welfare had a lot to do. The apparently incessant advance of industry brought serious social problems. Even to those who were not progressively minded, it was clear that large and densely packed populations needed policing and providing for in a way that old methods could not achieve. Meanwhile many of the old methods were still the only ones available. New problems and antiquated solutions made for a chaotic state of affairs. Improvement came slowly and sporadically. It took a long time for the burgh councils to assume active responsibility for the health and welfare of their citizens. Political reform edged on in steps through the century, but in the first half, at least, the urging and goading of national and local government by concerned individuals were more effectual than the ballot in procuring action. A royal commission examined the Scottish Poor Law in 1845, and responsibility for poor relief was transferred from kirk to state, with the establishment of nearly 800 parish boards. Glasgow was condemned as the most insanitary town in Britain in 1842, its slum population regularly ravaged by typhus, cholera and tuberculosis; by 1855 it had begun building the aqueducts that would bring pure water from Loch Katrine.

A New Railway System

Railways in Scotland had had a long history, beginning as gravity-worked industrial tramways running from collieries to nearby coastal ports. With the development of the steam locomotive, they quickly became important to industry. The first steam railway in the country ran from Kilmarnock to Troon, in Ayrshire, in 1817, though it was not until the Glasgow and Garnkirk line of 1831 that a truly effective steam railway could be said to exist, After that, continuing development was rapid. By 1842, Edinburgh and Glasgow were linked by rail; by 1850, it was possible to travel from Aberdeen to London by train. The world's first train-ferries went into action on the Firth of Forth.

The railways revolutionised inland transport with their bulk carrying capacity and their speed. Their unifying effect was very important. Newspapers and information could be distributed on a daily basis. Each burgh had formerly kept its own time; now with the railway timetable, a uniform time system had to be applied throughout the land. The distinctiveness of speech and custom of such regions as Buchan, Galloway and Fife were now starting to be eroded by population movement and by a trend – encouraged by nationally distributed newspapers and magazines – towards the standardisation of vocabulary. Many Scots words and provincial dialect expressions fell out of use – a process speeded up as a side-effect of the Education Act of 1872, which introduced compulsory free education for children between the ages of five and thirteen. Conforming to the curriculum of the London-based Scotch Education Department, teachers sought to eradicate 'uncouth' Scotticisms just as in the Highlands and Islands they forbade the use of Gaelic in classroom and playground.

A Religious Crisis

Once, for a time, Scotland had been a land ruled by its church, and this had never been forgotten. There were a number of reasons for the religious crisis of 1843. The prime one was the long-nursed resentment against patronage, but there were strong divisions within the kirk, between the 'moderates' and the less easy-going, more puritanical Presbyterians who believed that the ideals of the seventeenth century were being watered down. The success in the Protestant evangelisation of the Highlands encouraged this faction. Both parties could see that the kirk was not organised to cope with the new distribution of population. Some parishes were virtually empty of people; others were packed tight. And – to the concern of Presbyterians of all shades – a steady stream of immigrants from Catholic Ireland was entering Scotland, in the hope of earning a living. By 1841, over 15 per cent of the population of Glasgow were Catholic. This influx was one reason for removing poor relief from the church – the Catholic poor received short shrift from the Presbyterian beadles and deacons who doled out clothing, boots or bread.

To many churchmen, the kirk seemed to be increasingly marginalised in a materialistic epoch. At the general assembly of 1843, a variety of discontents crystallised in the Disruption, when 200 ministers, led by their moderator, walked out and set about founding the Free Church of Scotland. In a short time, 500 churches were built, manses were provided for the separatist ministers, and a new structure of independent church government was introduced. Congregations passed to the Free Church almost in their entirety, except for the laird and his family and those who were economically dependent on him. The established Church of Scotland kept three-fifths of its ministers and all its possessions. But its authority was deeply compromised. By the time a partial reunion was achieved in 1929, the secular British state was fully in control of welfare and education.

The Highland Clearances
The empty parishes, mentioned above, were most frequently found in the Highlands and Islands. The process of emigration and eviction, begun in the

previous century, gathered pace with ruthlessness and efficiency in the nineteenth. The kelp industry which, whatever its privations, had sustained the economy of many western areas, collapsed after 1815. The end of the Napoleonic Wars sharply reduced the demand for soldiers and sailors. There were few industries or usable natural resources in the Highlands, but still substantial populations lived at a subsistence level in their crude 'black houses' along the slopes of glens and straths, planting crops in the valley floors and herding cattle on the uplands. It was not, to the observer, a highly civilised lifestyle. One fastidious American compared Highland clachans to African kraals. But the Highlanders were not slaves to the regime of the factory siren. Many went south to do seasonal work, especially from the southern Highlands. To the modern-minded proprietor and his factor, educated in the best new principles of political economy and agricultural science and with a useful knowledge of land law, these inhabitants were an unwanted burden inherited from the past, and an obstacle to efficient use of the land. With help from police and military, every means at their disposal, from the relatively humane to the most brutal, was used to remove them permanently. Great tracts of the northern Highlands and entire islands were cleared of their people, and the organisation of emigration became an industry. The Highlanders had become heavily dependent on the potato and the potato blight of 1848–50, though it did not reach the catastrophic proportions of the Irish potato famine, added to their miseries.

The modernisers had put their trust in wool. Sheep replaced people, cattle and crops. But the march of progress betrayed them as it had others. The colonial sheep ranches of Australia, Argentina and New Zealand, assisted by fast steamships and the recently discovered technology of refrigeration, proved to be too competitive for the Highland sheep farms. From mid-century onwards, the Highlands were increasingly turned over to deer forest and grouse moor – a vast sporting enclave for the multiplying numbers of well-off industrialists who came up for the shooting season and, ironically, affected a form of the old Highland garb during their stay. The purchase of Balmoral Castle, on the River Dee, by Queen Victoria and Prince Albert in 1853, confirmed the rising status of the Highlands as holiday territory for the rich and super-rich. (The high point would be reached when Andrew Carnegie, the Scots-American steel-baron, built his dream-home at Skibo Castle, Sutherland, in the early 1900s.)

Industrial Relations
The distribution of population, at one time about even between Highlands and Lowlands, was now wholly distorted by industrial development and land clearance. By 1881, the population was 3,700,000, more than double that of 1801. Well over half lived in the narrow central area – Renfrewshire, Dunbartonshire, Lanarkshire, south Stirlingshire, East Lothian and Midlothian – which also encompassed the two cities of Glasgow and Edinburgh. The Highlands became an economically

and socially marginal area, removed from the political realities and priorities of the industrial zone.

Although a large part of the countryside under the 160-metre (500-foot) line was either under cultivation or good quality pasture, and farming was still labour-intensive – despite the introduction of mechanical reapers and threshers, and other steam-driven machinery – the essential concern of the densely populated belt and its two biggest urban out-stations, Dundee and Aberdeen, was with industry and commerce. The list of Scottish inventions, and improvements on inventions, in the nineteenth century is impressive, though other countries have their own lists too. The picture of inventive genius and entrepreneurial zeal needs to be tempered by the fact that much of the undoubted success of Scottish industry was based squarely on cheap labour. Materials were not necessarily to be had more cheaply than elsewhere: as industry grew more complex, much had to be imported. But Scottish workers had always accepted a low wage. By the later nineteenth century, the shocking and degrading (to modern eyes) working practices of the earlier decades had been dropped. The Education Act of 1872 provided that children under the age of fourteen should go to school, not to the factory (though many still did and even in 1875 it was still legal for those over ten to work). Women no longer worked as beasts of burden underground. Indeed the new demand for teachers and lady clerks offered women respectable salaried careers for the first time. The custom on farms of treating a labourer's wife or woman partner as an extra unpaid source of labour was abandoned. In many ways, social progress had improved the workers' way of life. But the Scottish proletariat was a low-paid one by the international standards of the time. The remarkable world dominance of shipbuilding on the Clyde was based on this as well on the engineering skills fostered in the shipyards and in city colleges and night-schools. The 'Jute Lords' of Dundee grew rich on the low pay rates offered to their workers (almost entirely women):

> Oh, dear me, the mill's gaun fest.
> And we poor shifters canna get oor
>   rest;
> Shiftin' bobbins, coorse and fine,
> There's little pleasure workin', for ten
>   and nine.

Although there were innovators, such as Sir Charles Parsons, developer of the steam turbine (1884), most factory owners were content to rely on established skills and existing machinery. Scottish industrialists were very slow to take up the challenge of the internal combustion engine: they still had plenty of coal (and North Sea oil was not even a dream). Such an industrial set-up, even if accepted by the majority of people (who often saw their escape in 'getting on', that is joining the managerial class, or in their children doing so) nevertheless provided fertile ground for trades unionism. Prior to 1850, all efforts to start unions had failed, and it was only in the second half of the century that, grudgingly, employers began to negotiate with workers' representative bodies such as the United Coal and Iron Miners' Association. The establishment of effective unions was not easy. Organised workers were regarded with suspicion and fear, and the climate of 'industrial relations' was a stormy one. In the early 1870s, a period which saw the highest rate of trade and industrial expansion, workers found that they had a market value which could be exploited. Pay rates rose, there were concessions on working hours (a 10-hour working day in 1875) and by 1880 a week-long holiday – usually without pay – was common. The Glasgow Fair, with its exodus of people on steamer trips down the Clyde and train excursions into the Highlands, became a summer institution. But these advances of the workers' interests were often accompanied by reversals. In 1891, railway workers rioted at Motherwell against the company's attempt to evict them from their 'tied' company houses. In 1894, 65,000 coal miners went on strike for five months, disrupting many other coal-dependent industries. A century before, miners had been little better than serfs, indentured workers compelled to live and work in the mining community (it was only in 1799 that the last restrictions were lifted). The old attitudes of employers died hard.

A New Political Party

From 1867, all adult males were eligible to vote, and this opened the way towards the formation of a workers' party. The Scottish Labour Party was founded in 1888 and merged with the Independent Labour Party in

1895. For several decades, however, the Liberal Party continued to dominate political life; indeed Scotland returned a majority of Liberal MPs in every election from 1832 to 1900. Scots were prominent in the formative years of the British Labour movement, its different strands effectively characterised by the dour and somewhat puritanical James Keir Hardie and the dashing, cavalierish Robert Cunninghame-Graham. Both found it easier to win seats in England; the focus of Labour activity was more on union organisation.

For the majority of Scots in the later nineteenth century, the Liberal Party seemed to fulfil their political aspirations. It stood for free trade and land reform, and also – not without internal division – for home rule. Although Ireland was the driving issue, Scottish home rule, meaning a degree of devolved government within the United Kingdom, was also part of the agenda. In 1886, the Liberal Party split on the issue of home rule for Ireland, and after that devolution became a lost cause. In Scotland, it was not a passionate issue, and the notion of national independence even less so; the Scots were still firmly imbued with the sense and spirit of the British Empire, with the 'old country' at its heart. In financial and commercial terms too, Scottish industry and Scottish banks were engaged with customers on a worldwide scale.

Land Reform
The question of land ownership and land reform was important. A few families owned most of the land and

natural resources of the country. Joseph Mitchell, the promoter and builder of the Highland Railway in the 1860s, remarked in his memoirs that: 'Although our kingdom contains upwards of three and a half millions of inhabitants, who are supposed from their education to be the most enlightened and intelligent people in Europe, yet they possess no interest in the territory of Scotland. One-half of their country is owned by seventy proprietors, while nine-tenths belongs to seventeen hundred persons.'

The focus of discontent was in the Highlands, where the land-holdings were largest. The surviving communities of Highlanders, whose old runrig system had been replaced by small individually tenanted crofts, had no security of tenure or rent. A Highland Land League was formed in 1882 to resist continuing enclosures of land and eviction of tenants, and a number of confrontations – the most famous being the 'battle of the Braes' on the Isle of Skye in 1882 – took place between crofters and the police and military. In 1883, the 'Crofters' War' was investigated by a royal commission, while hostilities went on. A gunboat with 250 marines was sent to Uig in Skye in 1884 to quell disturbances by inhabitants under threat of eviction. In 1886, the royal commission's work resulted in the provision of security of tenure, rent protection, and the establishment of the Crofters' Commission.

The Turn of the Century
Until very late in the century, the administration and

provision of services in Scotland's rural areas – outside the burghs – had been the responsibility and privilege of the landowners. In 1889, elected county councils were introduced, and if many of the same faces reappeared in the new councils, at least they had been elected. Public accountability made it less possible to be inert in such matters as the provision of roads, or corrupt in the handling of public money. Democracy was still some way off; women had no vote in parliamentary elections, and it was only in 1892 that the universities formally accepted women undergraduates (Edinburgh medical students had rioted in 1870 against women being allowed to attend anatomy lectures).

The end of the nineteenth century, marked by an unpleasant colonial war in South Africa, the 'Boer War', which aroused fiercely imperialist sentiment throughout the country, saw the identity of Scotland firmly equated with that of 'North Britain' – the northern extension of a wealthy, politically and socially advanced United Kingdom, hub of an empire of which Glasgow was proudly 'Second City' in size. Great Britain was more than a little complacent about its place in the world – a place that was generally considered, not least in Scotland, to be Number One.

CHAPTER TEN

Scotland in the Twentieth Century

The history of Scotland in the twentieth century, much of it well within living memory for most people, is of particular interest because a clear process can be seen and understood. The process is of external forces – events and pressures originating from outside Scotland and indeed often outside the United Kingdom – which in turn prompted internal responses within the country.

Briefly, these outside forces encompass the rise of a world trading system and of a worldwide instant communications network, the continuing advances in science and technology, the economic dominance of the United States of America, two world wars, the disappearance of the British empire, and the movement towards economic and political unity among the countries of western Europe.

As if it were some complex chemical compound undergoing a variety of tests in a laboratory, the reactions and side-effects can be observed and compared. Some of these reactions might be shared with other countries; others might be caused by the specifically Scottish nature of the society under test.

In the later nineteenth century, the country was imbued with a sense of being at the heart of an empire, of being the principal place the world came to for its ships and locomotives, of being at the centre of a network of commercial and financial relationships that stretched to the Far East, Latin America and East Africa. This conception of an imperial and industrial Scotland was so well established that it took a succession of severe shocks to kill it off, and it was not until the 1980s that it was finally laid to rest. The first of the shocks was the Great War of 1914–18.

World War I and Its Effects

The war brought a flush of prosperity to industry, helping to obscure the fact that much of the industrial plant was by now obsolescent. It brought higher pay to the workers and increased their strength in negotiation. Miners and engineers were widely condemned for wartime strikes, but they knew well that employers and landlords were making profits as never before, exploiting the opportunities of war without proposing to share the benefits, and without incurring the criticism directed at the workers.

It brought a new emancipation to women, whose mass participation in industry, especially in munitions-making, was crucial to army and naval supplies. At the fighting front, apocalyptic scenes were enacted during three years of military stalemate between vast, evenly matched forces, which ensured the massacre of millions of young men. Against this torrent of obliteration, certain myths exploded almost silently, including that of the international solidarity of the working class against capitalist-led warfare. For some, however, the

Russian Revolution of 1917–18 encouraged the belief that workers might triumph over a capitalist system.

Victory required, and was accorded, the participation of the United States of America on the allied side. Ten years later, the dominating importance and influence of the USA would have a negative effect when the Wall Street Crash of 1929 heralded an economic slump throughout the industrialised countries. In the intervening, immediate post-war years, Scottish society had to confront the legacy of the nineteenth century and World War I.

A post-war decline in coal prices and industrial output reduced the ability and urge to invest in modern machinery. Although there had been improvements in water supply and to a lesser degree in sanitation, the housing stock was largely of poor quality and ill-maintained, and the individual dwellings mostly too small and overcrowded to conform to acceptable standards at a time when social and medical criteria were beginning to be applied to such matters.

In other ways, change was faster. Motor transport and electric power were its main agents. Ease of transport and defeat of the dark began to transform life, especially in country areas. The dance hall, the cinema and the radio brought new aspects of entertainment into everyone's lives, at relatively low cost. Food manufacturing and distributing processes that had developed in wartime now changed civilian eating habits. Packaged goods with brand names encouraged people to regard themselves as consumers. This trend was assisted by greater sophistication in advertising, which was moving from plain information to more subtle forms of persuasion.

Such innovations raised people's expectations of what life could offer them, as the offerings of the new technological and commercial world became gradually more available and affordable. But for most people, other events, arising outside Scotland, delayed or diluted this consumerist trend over a period of 20 years.

The Depression

The slump of the early 1930s grew more severe, and job losses began to rise sharply. In 1932, unemployment was at an average of 27.7 per cent, a figure which conceals a much higher proportion in single-industry towns like the coal-mining community of Tranent or the iron-making one of Coatbridge. In addition, many people still in work had their wages cut by companies struggling to survive; employees of the state also suffered pay cuts. The depression was slower to end in Scotland than in some other parts of the United Kingdom, and in the 1930s there was considerable emigration of skilled workers into England and North Wales, where new industries were being established more rapidly. The process of recovery was painfully slow. By 1936, unemployment still averaged just under 19 per cent of the working population; in 1938 it was 16.3 per cent. By 1940, it had ceased to be a problem, but by then the advent of another world war had once again reinvigorated the industrial machine.

World War II

The first air raid of the war struck at the naval base of Rosyth in October 1939. Heavy raids on the lower Clyde in the spring of 1941 brought civilians into the front line: over 1,500 were killed. As in 1914–18, the war government instituted centralised control over many aspects of life. The entire region north of the Great Glen was a restricted area. Military airfields were set up along the east coast and at suitably level points in the west. With the German occupation of Norway in 1940, the 'circumpolar' position of Scotland became intensely strategic. Loch Ewe became an important base for the assembling of Atlantic convoys. Until the D-Day invasion of 1944, this war was much more one of air and sea, though many soldiers of the 51st Highland Division were captured in a rearguard action during the Dunkirk evacuation of 1942.

Like the 1914–18 war, World War II created and accelerated social change. Once again, women's work became a vital part of the war effort. New factories were set up to make munitions and war materials. Old factories were adapted to new needs. The Albion truck works made military vehicles. Shipyards worked intensively, both to replace the tonnage of merchant vessels lost in submarine attacks and to build warships. Virtually the whole population was mobilised or brought into the war effort in one way or another, from the children who collected metal pots and pans to be recycled into Spitfires, to the women who provided tea and buns for soldiers on the troop trains that ran up and down the country.

The Welfare State and Nationalised Industries

In the general election of 1945, following the surrender of Germany, a Labour Party was put in government at Westminster with a large majority. The result in Scotland reflected that in the rest of the United Kingdom. The social improvements that had been widely canvassed and anticipated during the wartime period, characterised as 'the Welfare State', were put in place, the one of prime importance to most people being the provision of a free National Health Service. Large parts of industry, government-controlled during the war, were now brought into national ownership – among them coal, steel, road haulage and the railways. By 1952, impatient with the continuation of many aspects of post-war austerity, including the rationing of clothes and sweets, United Kingdom voters returned the Conservatives to power.

While the Welfare State remained for several decades inviolate, the basic industries became a political football in the 1950s and 1960s, denationalised and sometimes re-nationalised by successive Conservative and Labour governments. In Scotland, their status was further complicated because the coal reserves were expensive to mine and not of the best quality; and the ironworks and steelworks were small, mostly old-fashioned, and inconveniently situated, especially for export markets. The railways were suffering from long-term under-investment, and many lines were unprofitable, though regarded as vital to the life and future development of the communities they served. But there was still apparent industrial vigour. In the mid-1950s, almost half a million tons of shipping was being launched each year on the Clyde; 20,000,000 tons of coal were being mined, 2,500,000 tons of steel were being produced, and almost a million tons of iron.

The Dismantling of the British Empire

At Maymyo, in the hills above Mandalay in Burma, there is a fine house called Candacraig. Now a government-owned hotel, it was built as a rest-and-recreation centre for the young men who came out from Scotland to work for the Bombay-Burmese Teak Company. Other pockets and larger communities of Scots could be found throughout the British empire – but the Scots have long since left Burma. The futile and humiliating French-British military adventure of 1965 when they attempted to retain control of the Suez Canal, underlined the degree to which British pretension by then lagged behind geopolitical realities.

The dismantling of the British empire was well under way. The independence of India in 1948 had been a pivotal moment. The Scots, having participated fully in the administration and commerce of the empire, found far less opportunity in the commonwealth that replaced it. The need for military manpower fell. The six Highland and eight Lowland regiments were subject to amalgamations and reductions in numbers and national military service for all males over 18 was abolished in 1960.

The Latter Half of the Twentieth Century

The bat-and-ball activity of British politicians on the home front in the 1950s did not prevent considerable modernisation and innovation in industry, but the dramatic regeneration of the devastated economies and industrial bases of Germany and Japan, and the huge increase in American manufacturing capacity, meant first of all a steady reduction in export business for Scottish heavy industry and, eventually, a vigorous assault from outside on the domestic market. For the consumer, this was a good thing. Through the 1950s, 60s and 70s, the Scots became increasingly able to acquire items that before the war had been unattainable except for the very rich – refrigerators, washing machines, television sets, motor cars, central heating. This was helped by changes in the financial industry – far more people had bank accounts, and hire purchase arrangements made it possible for people with regular incomes but no capital to buy expensive items. Many of these consumer items were made in Scotland, but the corporations which owned the factories were based outside the country and often outside the UK. Scotland-in-Britain was competing with other UK regions, and other countries, to attract 'inward investment', by offering strong incentives like ready-built factories, low rents and tax holidays.

The neglected and decrepit state of much Scottish housing had been acknowledged by the formation of the Scottish Special Housing Association in 1937; and was tackled more determinedly in the 1950s by a large building programme, sponsored by central government and much of it undertaken by town and county councils. The new pattern of housing extended from semi-detached and terraced houses – filling in empty spaces or replacing demolished buildings in towns and villages – to massive high-rise blocks on completely new sites on the outskirts of cities and larger towns. Until the 1980s, Scotland had one of the highest proportions of council house dwellers in Europe. Also during the 1950s, the process of extending sanitation and electrification throughout the country was continued.

By 1953, the year of the coronation of Queen Elizabeth II, most of the population lived within the range of television transmitters. Television studios were added to the BBC's centre in Glasgow, and Scottish programmes were made, picking up on the now-declining music hall tradition for the most part, but the new medium also helped to increase the quantitative impact of transatlantic and London-based culture. In 1957, the introduction of commercial television brought competition for the mass audience. By now, TV viewing was an established part of daily life. By the end of the century, the average family would spend almost the equivalent of a day a week in front of the small screen. To this could be added time spent using personal computers, using the Internet as a source of information and entertainment as well as, increasingly, a means of doing business. Scotland was a district of the global village, which enforced its own cultural conditions and protocols.

In Europe – the continent responsible for originating the century's two world wars, and with a notorious record for political instability and mutual hostility between its neighbouring nations – something remarkable took place during the 1960s. The ancient enemies drew together in an economic and political union, creating both a trading power and an internal market that could rival the two world super-powers, the USA and the Soviet Union. In 1972, the United Kingdom became a member of the European Community (later the European Union).

In 1975, there was a referendum on membership, with a majority of Scots voting in favour (only the Northern and Western Isles recorded a majority against). From then on, Westminster was no longer the ultimate place of decision for many aspects of economic, social and legal life. Brussels and Strasbourg became significant places.

Within the political life of the United Kingdom, a new strain of Conservative thinking became apparent in the late 1970s. Loosely labelled 'Thatcherism' after Mrs Margaret Thatcher who became prime minister in 1979, it was distinguished by a strong belief in the virtue of competition, and in the ability of market forces to create a satisfactory basis for social life. The 'nannying' aspects of the Welfare State were attacked. Councils were first encouraged, then compelled, to sell off their houses (200,000 were sold by 1990), transport systems, and other amenities. Virtually all remaining publicly owned businesses were privatised, and subsequently went through a process of rationalisation which normally involved reduction of staff and closure of inefficient or remote plants and depots. In 1975, local government was reorganised into nine large regions – an initiative which was amended in 1994 by the setting-up of 28 'unitary' authorities. An important part of Thatcherism was the reduction of the power and influence of trades unions. The years of Conservative rule between 1979 and 1997 had a strong impact on the political life and economy of Scotland. An industrial counter-revolution took place in those latter decades of the twentieth century. The older 'smokestack' industries were toppled, literally and metaphorically. Apart from some open-cast coal mining, the industries which had typified Scotland for more than a hundred years are now non-existent. Just as the coal mines were being shut down, it became clear that huge oil and natural gas reserves lay in strata far below the bed of the North Sea, and as prices of Middle East crude oil rose, so the exploitation of the offshore fields became possible. In 1984, the North Sea was the world's fifth most productive oilfield. But the oil and gas business needed only a small fraction of the numbers who had been employed digging coal, and observers noted that the revenues from 'Scottish' oilfields did not remain in Scotland.

Between 1979 and 1992, four out of ten manufacturing jobs in the country ceased to exist. Unemployment rose to a maximum level of between 9 and 10 per cent, around a quarter of a million people, in 1993. Though much below the 1930s level, the average figures again conceal blight in individual places, such as the former coal-mining town of Dalmellington in Ayrshire. Service industries expanded greatly, and in 1992 more than

220,000 people were employed in the financial sector – more than had ever been employed in the coalfields. Many of these jobs were for women and often on a part-time basis.

These twentieth-century events and developments were hammer-blows that struck hard at the life of the nation; or to change the metaphor, they were powerful reshaping agents which forced a traditionally minded community out of inertia and into a fit state to respond to the opportunities and difficulties of the twenty-first century. How did the Scots react to this succession of disaster and stimulus?

Looking Back on the Twentieth Century

The certainties of one generation become increasingly hollow until they form the myths of those which follow; and finally expire altogether in apathy or derision. In the early years of the twentieth century, up until around 1916, there were some strong certainties at the basis of life for most Scots. The key-stones of the structure were the British empire, a Protestant God, and the perception of the country as one of the world's main engine-rooms of material progress. From needles and pins to high-pressure boilers, Scotland was a maker of the artefacts of the modern industrial world. This view, held by most people, was the traditionalist one – with the recent tradition of a community engaged in heavy industry grafted on to an older sense of social order, of religion and of dynastic loyalty. A degree of complacency inevitably emerged from this, as did a fear of and hostility to change. The Forth Bridge, completed in 1890, rugged, massive, imposing, built to last, was the physical manifestation of this certainty, just as the first Tay Bridge of 1878, which collapsed in 1879, had demonstrated the shoddiness of attitude and workmanship that could also be contained within it.

Uncomfortably yoked with the traditionalists were the people who formed the critical or reformist section of Scottish society. For a variety of reasons they set their minds against some or all of the certainties shared by their fellow-citizens. In the early years of the century, these reasons were largely social and economic. The reformists were largely engaged within the trades union movement and the small groups which would coalesce into the Labour Party. They canvassed a wide range of solutions, but the key-stone of their beliefs was that wealth within the country was distributed unfairly, and that a small number of people should not be in a position to exploit a very much larger number. They too had a sense of history, and looked far back to an idealised tribal past when 'the people' owned the land. Among the reformists there was also a belief that 'home rule' for Scotland was desirable, though this was a secondary theme for politicians who had grown up in the context of the United Kingdom and whose political mentors had taught reliance on the internationalism of the working class as the means of achieving their social aims.

Both these groups were terribly shaken by the war of 1914–18 and its mass destruction of human lives, and of the prosperity that could be based upon such carnage. From it, the reformists emerged strengthened, encouraged at first also by the Soviet revolution. (The Glasgow socialist, John Maclean, was named as the revolutionary government's consul; the British government subsequently put him in jail for sedition.) The beliefs of the traditionalist element were somewhat weakened. The attrition of the trenches and the indecisive naval battle of Jutland in 1915 undermined the sense of British invincibility nurtured since the days of Wellington and Nelson. Faith in empire was shaken; the Americans were sharply hostile to British or other imperialism, and the peace treaty broke up the empires of Europe. And the Protestant God (who was also the God of the Germans) had been offered a holocaust of the best of the nation's youth to no obvious purpose.

In the post-war years, the spirit of the nation became more secular. Even in 1910, the kirk's general assembly had deplored the reduction in the numbers of children attending Sunday School. Now the new mobility and new forms of entertainment made it easier for a new generation to enjoy itself without being under censorious eyes, and the new emphasis on consumerism encouraged a materialist view of life. The union in 1929 of the Church of Scotland and the United Free Church, partially healing the Disruption of 1843, did not herald a religious revival. Once upon a time, it could have been claimed that the kirk's general assembly was more representative of the nation than the parliament. Now the levers of social reform were in the hands of politicians, many of whom were Catholics or agnostics, and the kirk was a respected but powerless influence, maintaining a long, slow and ultimately losing campaign against the decline of the people's belief into religious apathy. Encouraged by the rise of Labour as a governing party – headed by a Scot, James Ramsay Macdonald – the reformist element was active in promoting social policy. In the 1920s, with the Labour Party clearly focused on all-British politics, those who believed strongly in self-government set up their own parties, including the Scots National League (1921) whose aim was for complete independence, not simply home rule. From now on, Scottish nationalism would be a consistent, though for several decades still minor, strand of political life.

Nationalists were a tiny though often vocal minority of the population of five million now inhabiting the land. Traditional attitudes still prevailed at all levels of society. Working conditions in mines, mills, shipyards and factories remained often primitive and dangerous. Under a Labour government in 1924, a Scottish MP, John Wheatley, introduced a Housing Act which enforced minimum standards. The imposition of new standards for house-building did not promote new construction, and many people opted to pay less and stay in the damp tubercular tenement (even if they could afford to do otherwise). These were not purely urban problems; they afflicted small towns and even farm cottages just as much. A more typically urban phenomenon was the death of infants. Childhood diseases such as rickets, caused by malnutrition, were prevalent – ignorance and apathy among parents contributed to this.

As the rocky economic conditions of the 1920s gave way to outright slump in 1930, the sense of an industrial nation was replaced by the vision of a nation on the dole. Just as the generals of 1914–18 could not find their way to victory out of a bloody stalemate, so the politicians and economists of the 1930s could not find a way out of the 'Great Depression'. But in these desperate times, there was little active protest. The industrial workers of Scotland were used to enduring hard times, and it was plain to all that the situation was little different in other countries. Even the old recourse of emigration was removed, with the one-time lands of promise themselves in the grip of slump. Empire, kirk, king, industry had no power to alter things. One of the consequences of the Depression was to emphasise to individuals their personal helplessness in the grip of economic events far beyond their control, and manifestly beyond the control of the government. What was the good of being a consumer when there was no money to buy anything? A more positive result of the enforced leisure was to sharpen city dwellers' awareness of the wild countryside only a short distance away. Young Glaswegians taught themselves mountaineering techniques in what they christened the 'Arrochar Alps', and the Scottish Youth Hostels Association was started in 1931. Awareness of the Highlands as one of Europe's great 'wilderness' regions brought new visitors who were unwelcome to many landowners intent on keeping people out of their empty acres of deer forest.

During the 1930s, the desire for an improved society,

with more to offer to all its citizens by way of wealth, security and material possessions, grew stronger. It was driven not only by people's reactions to the slump but also by the desire to see a more equal society. The techniques of industry and business, now encompassing mass-production and mass-persuasion, renewed the push towards the concept of a nation of consumers. New 'light' industries began producing household goods at relatively low prices. The chain-store became familiar, with names like Lipton's (for groceries) and the 'Fifty-Shilling Tailors' appearing on new buildings along town high streets. Mass-produced small cars like the Baby Austin and Ford Ten extended the range of car ownership beyond the wealthy. Alongside such political and economic trends, a serious, if spasmodic and sometimes incoherent, debate was going on. It related not so much to the state of the nation's wealth as the state of the nation's soul. A number of prominent journalists and authors explored this issue, among them William Power in *Scotland and the Scots,* Edwin Muir in *Scottish Journey,* Lewis Grassic Gibbon and Hugh MacDiarmid in *Scottish Scene.* Widely varying both in their intentions and their perceptions, they nevertheless focused the attention of their readers on Scotland, as a specific country, and the Scots, as a particular people. Many who took no interest in political nationalism read, and were influenced by, these books. The indirect message was that Scotland had distinctive attributes, which needed to be preserved in order to satisfy a deep-felt need of the Scottish people. For similar reasons, in these years, the National Trust for Scotland was founded (1930), and the Saltire Society (1936). The 'Little Houses' movement, beginning in Crail and dedicated to the preservation and regeneration of Scots vernacular architecture, also dates from this time. Most of this was common ground both to traditionalists and to reformists, though the country's two leading poets had a celebrated spat in the mid-30s over the use of the Scots language as a literary medium, and the degree to which Scotland could be said to have a major literary tradition. Hugh MacDiarmid, more combative than Edwin Muir, fought a war of words in favour of 'Lallans' (broad Scots – a form developed by modern Scottish writers); Muir, less engaged, essentially took the view that the Scots are co-owners of the English language, and both share in, and have strongly contributed to, its tradition.

By 1939, reformist and traditionalist could also share a common goal in fighting the new war against Germany. However, the experience of World War I, and the intervening years, had significantly changed attitudes. A seemingly instinctive and unthinking patriotism had filled the ranks in 1914 and 1915 (conscription was introduced in 1916). But at the beginning of World War II, most waited for their conscription papers. There was far greater awareness of what the war was about. Most different was the strong sense of what needed to be done once victory had been accomplished. Reformism was no longer a minority pursuit. A return to the conditions of the 1920s and 30s was repugnant to the great majority of people. The demand for social change was urgent, and in the case of Scotland, change began even in the course of the war. Thomas Johnston, the Secretary of State for Scotland in the wartime coalition government, set up the North of Scotland Hydro-Electric Board as a state-owned enterprise with a specific social remit to bring the benefits of electrification even to the remotest and smallest communities.

Waging all-out war fostered a spirit of British national unity and resolve. The sense of the entire post-war United Kingdom requiring to be modernised into a country providing a decent standard of living and acceptable levels of opportunity for all its inhabitants was a powerful one which had the effect of sidelining and diminishing a specifically Scottish nationalism. For 20 years or so after World War II, Scotland and England broadly shared the same political consensus, and the same broad division of Labour and Tory votes between working-class towns and cities, on the one hand, and middle-class suburbs and farming counties on the other. There was a curious episode in 1949 when John McCormick, a prominent nationalist, organised the Scottish Covenant, an appeal for a Scottish parliament, which was signed by over a million people. It had no effect at all.

During the 1950s, the country displayed aspects both of the past and the future. It was only in 1957 that the horse-breeding grant to farmers was abolished, spelling the final end of the farm horse. In that year, commercial television was established and the Hunterston nuclear power station begun. Work also began on the giant new steelworks at Ravenscraig, Motherwell (to be shut down and razed in 1992). Tradition and reform still pulled in their conflicting directions. But so much reform had been accomplished that many reforms were now part of the 'traditional' landscape. As much reformist energy went into protecting what had been achieved as in setting out new goals. In 1955, for the first and only time between 1945 and the end of the century, the Conservative-Unionists had a majority of Scottish seats (36 to Labour's 32). The Liberals had a solitary stronghold in Orkney and Shetland. To the traditionalists, the old staples that had reassured their grandparents were still present, though none were unscathed. Empire was dramatically reduced by the loss of India; the monarchy had become controversial with the accession of the new queen in 1952, designated Elizabeth II in Scotland though Scotland had never had an Elizabeth I. The established church was engrossed in an internal debate about whether it should have bishops or not, while the preoccupations of the people continued to grow ever more secular. The traditional Scottish Sunday, when everything was closed, was still maintained, but pressures for relaxation were becoming stronger, and the congregations of all the Protestant churches were dwindling. Industry still throbbed, rattled and smoked. But by 1958, the closure of many coal mines was being forecast, and the advance order books of shipbuilding companies were becoming increasingly thin. As the outlook for heavy industry grew bleaker, industrial relations, always a tricky field for the Scots, became stormier. This was typified by the angry confrontations that took place in the remaining Clyde shipyards in the 70s and in the coalminers' strike of 1984. As the real industries passed into memory, so the industrial museum arose – fisheries at Anstruther, mining at Dalkeith, the cloth mills at New Lanark, steam railways at Brechin and various other places. Some observers criticised the rise of a 'museum culture', but there was a real need for such places. Much that was familiar was disappearing from the scene and people felt a psychological need to preserve something of what had until so recently been central to the fabric of their lives. Even the traditional industries that survived – whisky, tweed-making, agriculture – were much changed and required far fewer workers.

Change had been equally dramatic and far-reaching in the nineteenth century, but then for the most part it had been viewed as positive – generating wealth and benefits. By the 1960s, change was being identified with decline and uncertainty rather than with progress. Virtually nothing remained of the once-great British empire. Great Britain was an offshore island of Europe, its political and economic influence much reduced. At times, as in 1976, its economy seemed on the verge of collapse. The painful adjustment of perspective and attitude revealed the degree to which a British ethos had been the product of empire and world war. Now it became clear that old lines of cleavage remained.

From the early 1960s, a political divergence between

England and Scotland became increasingly marked. Each successive government, whether Labour or Conservative, was making efforts to introduce new industry to replace the old companies now going into liquidation. In 1961, trucks were being built at Bathgate, and a car factory was announced for Linwood; a big wood-pulp mill was set up at Corpach, by Fort William. Despite such instances of inward investment, there was a sense of commercial decline: many businesses were closing down or being bought up by international companies. In 1963, only vigorous protests from every element in the community prevented the railways north of Inverness being closed, but many other lines throughout the country were shut down. External forces and agencies again seemed, as in the 1930s, to have the country at their mercy. The political anxiety and uncertainty resulting from this came sharply into focus with a Scottish National Party by-election victory at Hamilton, a supposed Labour fortress, in 1967. In successive general elections, divergent voting patterns in Scotland and England affected the result in each country; in 1970, a large Labour majority in Scotland was eclipsed by a large Tory majority in England; in the two elections of 1974, the Scottish Labour majority enabled Labour to take power despite narrowly losing in England. (October 1974 also saw 11 Nationalist MPs elected.) Between 1979 and 1997, ever-greater Labour majorities in Scotland were nullified in the Westminster parliament by substantial Tory wins in England. The implication was clear, that the market and monetarist philosophy espoused by the Tories under Margaret Thatcher was not palatable to most Scots. Traditionalists and reformists alike were in favour of a directed economy with an element of public ownership; indeed the real *reformistas* emerged as the small but vocal band of Scottish Conservatives who fully endorsed Thatcherist politics. One of them, Sir Teddy Taylor, unfavourably compared the effect of state aid given to Upper Clyde Shipbuilders with dropping millions of £10 notes from an aeroplane above Glasgow.

The centre-point of political debate in Scotland was several degrees to the left of that in England. Whether a new focus on devolution arose because of that fact, or because of the sense that Conservative governments were governing Scotland against the people's expressed will, is debatable, and probably both played a part. Despite great reluctance on the part of Labour, and the indifference of the Conservatives, devolution began to be a significant issue. The European referendum of 1975, with community membership decisively supported, also played a part. The concept of Scotland-in-Europe was altogether different from that of Scotland-on-its-own, which still frightened a majority of voters. A referendum on devolution, held in 1979, and requiring the assent of more than 40 per cent of the electorate (as distinct from 50 per cent of the voters) failed to reach the necessary level of support, and the issue was buried at Westminster though not at home. The 1997 general election returned no Tory MPs at all from Scotland. The new Labour government held a referendum on devolution which delivered a handsome majority in favour of a parliament, and a slightly smaller one in favour of giving this parliament limited tax-varying powers. In May 1999, the first elections for the new parliament, using a carefully worked out proportional representation system which allowed for nominated as well as directly elected members, saw Labour as the largest party, but lacking an overall majority. A Labour-Liberal Democrat coalition formed the 'Executive' (the word 'government' was studiously avoided).

After an uncertain start, the Scottish parliament and Executive began to employ the powers granted to them. Scotland ratified the European Convention on Human Rights a year before England and Wales did. The leftward trend of social policy was underlined by decisions to abolish tuition fees for Scottish students in Scottish universities and colleges, and to explore the possibility of free care for old age pensioners – both policies at variance with those of the Labour government at Westminster. The untimely death in October 2000 of Donald Dewar, the first First Minister, who had overseen the whole process of the referendum and the inception of the Scottish parliament, was a shock. But it showed the significance of the office as well as of the man. By the end of the year 2000, the role of the Scottish parliament was an accepted part of the fabric of national life.

CHAPTER ELEVEN

Twenty-first Century Scotland

The ten-yearly population census made in 2001 enabled the Scots to take stock of themselves and their nation at the beginning of a new century and millennium. The returns established the population at 5,062,011, just over 40,000 less than ten years previously. Of these, 48.05 per cent were male and 51.95 per cent female. Just over a third, 36.66 per cent, were under 30 years of age. Two per cent described themselves as non-white; and 1.16 per cent claimed some ability to speak Gaelic. Just over two-thirds, 67.91 per cent, considered themselves to be in good health, and 148,082 were unemployed. More than a quarter of the working population, 27.28 per cent, were on the public payroll, in healthcare, teaching, or administration. The largest single category of employed person was in manufacturing, at 13.65 per cent, but wholesale and retail trading was running it very close, at 13.3 per cent. Certain old staples, such as mining and fishing, had all but vanished at 1.9 per cent (including quarrying) and 0.31 per cent respectively. Of the country's 2,192,246 households, almost a third, 32.88 per cent, consisted of only a single person. Most were owner occupied, at 62.59 per cent, but council-rented property still accounted for 21.57 per cent of homes, despite 20 years of effort from central governments to reduce it. Almost two thirds of households had a car or van at their disposal, but 34.23 per cent did not.

Fewer Babies, Fewer People

In many ways this was a very different picture to 1901 or even 1951 or 1971. In a country increasingly subject to rapid change, and very much part of the Internet and World Wide Web community, there were, however, certain stubborn features which remained, including quite a high proportion of people feeling themselves to be in poor health. Scotland continued to have an exceptionally high, though decreasing, level of heart disease and strokes compared with other European countries. Politicians and economists were concerned by the steadily falling birth rate. In 1971, 66,500 babies were born in Scotland; in 2001, the number was 51,642. Women were having fewer children, and giving birth at a later stage in their lives, than in earlier decades. Combined with emigration, often of highly qualified young people, and a low level of immigrant arrivals, the demographers' forecast was of a continuing slow but steady diminution of the population. But few social changes occur in isolation, and this trend was closely linked to the very large number of women at work, accounting for half the labour force. Very many Scottish households required two incomes to maintain the level of expenditure and consumption that were possible in a developed economy.

By the time a second parliament was elected, in May 2003, a degree of apathy was apparent among voters.

Over half, 51.6 per cent, did not bother to vote. A number of significant parliamentary acts, including the Land Reform Bill of 2003, picked up on concerns that had been neglected, in some cases, for over a hundred years, and showed that the Scottish parliament was tackling at least some substantial issues. But great anger and a sense of national embarrassment was generated by the escalating cost of the new parliament building. When finally opened by Queen Elizabeth on 9 October 2004, its cost had risen from an estimate of £40 million to an actual £450 million, in less than five years. An inquiry found there was 'no single villain' but the evident incompetence and loud self-exculpation of highly paid persons aroused widespread resentment.

Issues for Scots

A great deal has been done to modernise the 'infrastructure' of Scotland – roads, railways and airports. In 2009, many town centres have changed dramatically, with the restoration of old buildings and large pedestrian zones. But the effect is still patchy, and many of the new developments seem charmless or impersonal. The marriage of tradition and modernity seems hard to bring off successfully in Scotland, and the nature and desirability of development remains a controversial issue. Also, looking ahead, a critical situation can be seen developing as more of the population move into older age groups, requiring more in the way of medical and social care. Cost is only one issue – another is where will all the carers come from? Another concern is the country's ability to assimilate new immigrants, of disparate racial and cultural backgrounds. Even Anglo-Saxons have sometimes complained about meeting more than semi-humorous prejudice. Within the different contexts of the United Kingdom, the enlarged European community, and the wider political, trading and financial world, many Scottish 'institutions', whether banks, friendly societies, or infantry regiments, are under threat of amalgamation or dissolution.

Other global concerns impinge on Scotland, including those of global warming and rising sea levels. Densely populated areas round the Clyde and Forth estuaries, in particular, are under long-term threat. Despite the discovery of further oil and gas fields in the Atlantic, the high point of oil production has passed, and exploitation of new fields, in deep and stormy waters, will only be possible if the price of crude oil remains high – which in itself has implications for the Scottish economy, especially in remote and island areas. Yet Scotland, well-endowed with wind, tides and water, and with little prospect of drought, is fortunately placed as a source of renewable power generation and fresh water supply.

In the European elections of 2004, the SNP saw its vote much reduced, though it retained two Euro-MPs. It was a different story in the general election of 2007.

General Election 2007

On Thursday 3 May 2007 the third general election to elect members to the Scottish Parliament saw the Scottish National Party emerge, albeit by the narrowest of margins, as the largest party, with 47 seats. Scottish Labour followed with 46 seats. The Scottish Conservatives won 17 seats, the Scottish Liberal Democrats 16 seats, the Scottish Green Party two seats and Margo MacDonald (Independent) was also elected.

Previously an energetic addition to the debate of the Parliament, the Scottish Socialist Party lost all their seats. Tommy Sheridan's new party, Solidarity, also failed to win any seats. The Scottish Senior Citizens Unity Party lost their seats. Campbell Martin and Dr Jean Turner both lost their seats, and Dennis Canavan and Brian Monteith retired.

The main issues during the campaign trail were healthcare, education, council tax reform, Trident and the Iraq War. Voters who may have supported the more minor opposition parties in the last election seemed now to turn to the SNP. While the protest vote was certainly a feature of this election, the SNP fought a strong campaign and Alex Salmond was a credible leader.

Rejected Ballots

Rejected ballots were a key feature of this general election – 142,000 of them. The reasons for the confusion surrounding the ballot papers are varied. The ballot papers for the constituency elections were combined with those for the regional lists. An instruction at the top of each form stated 'you have two votes', and many voters used both votes on parties in the regional list. Voters were given two papers with two different voting systems – one for the parliamentary election where voters were meant to use a cross, and one for local councils where they showed their preference with numbers. This was also the first British election where electronic counting of papers had taken place. There was a suggestion that had they been scrutinised by eye far fewer would have been rejected. During the BBC's live election coverage, as the extent of the spoiled papers became apparent, BBC Scotland's then political editor Brian Taylor described the situation as 'a disgrace'.

Unity from Minority

While the ballot controversy still raged, the practicalities of forming a government remained. Salmond was elected First Minister with Nicola Sturgeon as deputy, as well as Secretary for Health and Wellbeing.

The Liberal Democrats declined to form a coalition with the SNP. The Scottish National Party did not attempt to force any other coalition alliances and formed a minority government.

Thus has begun an exceptionally interesting period in Scottish politics. Budgets and bills must be passed with the true cooperation of the other parties. And while the usual political backbiting and points-scoring inevitably continue, a more unified approach to problem solving is the only successful way forward.

Scottish Labour, having seen its membership starting to fall, have had to rethink their previously close connection with New Labour at Westminster and revisit what makes Scottish Labour appeal to Scottish people. However, although it has been said that Scottish nationalism may still not be at the forefront of voters' reasons for voting SNP, the party have formed a credible government and have had an energetically productive time in office, despite ministerial lack of experience. The Nationalists have discovered the power they can wield from mere devolution.

Gordon Brown became UK Prime Minster in June 2007 and for the first time in the modern Scottish Parliament's short history, rival parties were forced to cooperate in the running of Scotland. The funding of Scotland within the United Kingdom government became, not for the first time, a controversial issue. Brown risked losing more Scottish voters by not cooperating with Holyrood's budget needs, and yet resentment from English voters was becoming more vocal. The Barnett Formula, which decides spending per head of Scots population was crticised often during this period. Scottish journalists countered this criticism by detailing Scotland's not insubstantial contribution to the UK, especially via oil revenues. Whether real or media manufactured, perceived Scottish and English rivalries made news items.

Recession

The extent to which the worldwide economic downturn, which began in 2008, will affect Scotland is beginning to show, with bankruptcies, job losses and business closures, not to mention our crippled banking system, already hitting headlines. How it will affect how Scotland votes remains to be seen.

In the July 2008 Glasgow East by-election the SNP increased their vote by 26 per cent to win the seat from Labour. A month later they did not fare quite so well in Glenrothes. However, their share of the vote increased by 13 per cent. Labour retained a formerly safe Labour seat, but by a very narrow margin, and with a decrease in percentage share of the vote.

Time will tell whether, in times of economic crisis, the trend for political change will persist or whether voters will go back to long-held, seemingly safer, allegiances.

The Scottish people should rightly fear the worst from this time of recession. With Britain's public finances facing their biggest crisis since 1931, and with debts soaring, it has been predicted that Scotland will suffer worst within the UK. The downturn in manufacturing, matched by a downturn in services and public sector jobs means lean times are ahead for Scottish workers.

Yet even in these lean times, there has been a discernable and much needed boost to the forging of a better Scottish national identity: the 'Executive' is now known as the Scottish Government; the Scottish Parliament's credibility has done nothing but grow; Alex Salmond is an articulate and statesmanlike leader; there is renewed interest in St Andrew's Day, Robert Burns and reaching out to other countries through Tartan Day and Homecoming, as well as the forthcoming 2014 Commonwealth Games in Glasgow.

Times are undoubtedly tough, but, over the centuries, Scotland and her people have certainly survived worse.

Index

187